WHO KNOWS:

Information in the Age of the Fortune 500

COMMUNICATION AND INFORMATION SCIENCE
A Series of Monographs, Treatises, and Texts

Edited by
MELVIN J. VOIGT
University of California, San Diego

William C. Adams • Television Coverage of the Middle East
Hewitt D. Crane • The New Social Marketplace: Notes on Effecting Social Change in America's Third Century
Rhonda J. Crane • The Politics of International Standards: France and the Color TV War
Herbert S. Dordick, Helen G. Bradley, and Burt Nanus • The Emerging Network Marketplace
Glen Fisher • American Communication in a Global Society
Edmund Glenn • Man and Mankind: Conflict and Communication Between Cultures
Bradley S. Greenberg • Life on Television: Content Analyses of U.S. TV Drama
John S. Lawrence and Bernard M. Timberg • Fair Use and Free Inquiry: Copyright Law and the New Media
Robert G. Meadow • Politics as Communication
William H. Melody, Liora R. Salter, and Paul Heyer • Culture, Communication, and Dependency: The Tradition of H.A. Innis
Vincent Mosco • Broadcasting in the United States: Innovative Challenge and Organizational Control
Kaarle Nordenstreng and Herbert I. Schiller • National Sovereignty and International Communication: A Reader
Dallas W. Smythe • Dependency Road: Communications, Capitalism, Consciousness and Canada
Herbert I. Schiller • Who Knows: Information in the Age of the Fortune 500

In Preparation:
William C. Adams • Television Coverage of the 1980 Presidential Campaign
William C. Adams • Television Coverage of International Affairs
Mary B. Cassata and Thomas Skill • Life on Daytime Television
Ithiel de Sola Pool • Forecasting The Telephone: A Retrospective Technology Assessment
Oscar H. Gandy, Jr. • Beyond Agenda Setting: Information Subsidies and Public Policy
Bradley S. Greenberg • Mexican Americans and the Mass Media
Cees J. Hamelink • Finance and Information: A Study of Converging Interests
Robert M. Landau, James H. Bair, Jean H. Siegman • Emerging Office Systems
Vincent Mosco • Pushbutton Fantasies
Kaarle Nordenstreng • The Mass Media Declaration of UNESCO
Dan Schiller • Telematics and Government
Jorge A. Schnitman • Dependency and Development in the Latin American Film Industries
Indu B. Singh • Telecommunications in the Year 2000: National and International Perspectives
Jennifer D. Slack • Communication Technologies and Society: Conceptions of Causality and the Politics of Technological Intervention
Janet Wasko • Movies and Money: Financing the American Film Industry
Osmo Wiio • Information and Communication Systems

WHO KNOWS:

INFORMATION IN THE AGE OF THE FORTUNE 500

by
Herbert I. Schiller
University of California, San Diego

 ABLEX Publishing Corporation, Norwood, New Jersey

Printed in the United States of America.
Library of Congress Cataloging in Publication Data

Schiller, Herbert I., 1919-
  Who knows.
  (Communication and information science)
  Includes bibliographical references and indexes.
  1. Communication—United States. 2. Communication,
International. 3. Communication—Economic aspects.
I. Title. II. Series.
P92.U5S3   001.5   81-3572
ISBN 0-89391-069-4   AACR2

ABLEX Publishing Corporation
355 Chestnut Street
Norwood, New Jersey 07648

For Anita

ACKNOWLEDGEMENTS

In New York, I was helped immeasurably by Elizabeth and Stuart Ewen. I derived much pleasure from their company and benefitted from their critical insights. Robert Stanley at Hunter College was a strong source of support. Donna Mancuso was a great assistant. Karen Kearns was a good friend. Jim Aronson was the best of office mates.

Extra-continental assistance and encouragement—and here I am sure I make many inadvertent omissions—came from the Latin American Institute for Transnational Studies (ILET), in Mexico City. Within that organization, Juan Somavia, Fernando Reyes Matta, Noreen Janus and Rafael Roncagliolo were especially helpful. Cees Hamelink, in the Institute of Social Studies in The Hague, at all times, offered collegial and critical comment. G. Russell Pipe generously assisted me with documentation. Edmund Hogrebe widened my understanding of many questions. Kaarle Nordenstreng was a distant but important informational and human asset, as were James D. Halloran and Enrique Gonzalez Manet.

I hope my many good friends in the Department of Film and Theatre at the University of Stockholm and in Swedish Broadcasting will understand and accept an overall acknowledgement of their gracious assistance during the time I was living in Stockholm and was starting out on this project. I must mention the special contributions of Karl-Ole Nilsson, Jan Ekecrantz, Nils Hugo Geber, Gören Hedebro and Margareta Ingelstam.

In California, many colleagues and friends read and commented on parts of the manuscript. I thank Robert Meadow, Robert Jacobson, Jerry DiMolis and Paul Zarins for carefully reviewing individual chapters. Melvin Voigt, editor of the Ablex Communication and Information Sciences Series, helped out all along the way and I am especially grateful to him. Eileen Mahoney assisted me with my classroom responsibilities while I was working on the manuscript. She offered also spirited criticism of the work-in-progress.

There is no way I can properly credit the contributions of Anita, Dan, and Zach Schiller to this work. They were involved at every stage of the project, discussing the basic conceptions and giving me their thinking, as well as criticizing my own.

Alma Salcido and Gail Cecil did considerable typing, taking time from many other tasks. I thank them.

Herbert I. Schiller

CONTENTS

INTRODUCTION

The business pages of daily newspapers are filled with accounts of the launching of new communication satellites, of cable TV franchises being granted by cities to this or that corporate conglomerate, of the latest *IBM* computer's number-crunching capability, and of the widening home market for electronic products and systems. (Almost a million home video recording instruments were sold in 1980.)

No longer only a prospect on the horizon, Americans and the American economy visibly, palpably, are engulfed in new communication technologies, processes, systems, and products. Some industrial workers, in their plants, find themselves on the line next to computerized robots. Office staff sit in front of the display panels of their word-processing machines for hours on end. Children accumulate micro-processor operated toys and games. Many of us watch television fed from a satellite into a cable system into our homes, possibly soon to bypass the cable intermediary, and be transmitted directly into our home sets.

The possible consequences of these remarkable developments often receive more extravagant interpretation than the actual changes. The designation of the era as an "information age" is one of the more modest descriptions applied to what is going on. More imaginative minds believe that the changes resulting from the new technology signify nothing less than the transcendence of capitalism itself. One currently popular view claims that what is emerging is an individualized, electronic, global commune, some of it in space and all of it ecologically focused.

Still another category of analysis stresses the appearance of a "post-industrial" society, in which knowledge workers and technocratically trained managers are committed to controlling the content of their work and the character of their work environment. These professionals are concerned also, according to this reading of the times, with producing objects and services of inherent worth.

Leaving aside what may or may not be possible, what is actually and verifiably changing in the informational condition of American society? This constitutes the central focus of this work. It has necessitated looking at the specific details of organizational structures, governmental and private; examining a few of the many new institutional arrangements designed for information production and dissemination in the corporate and public sectors; and, outlining some of the legal, legislative and industrial procedures under which new communication technologies are invented, introduced and made operational.

If there is an overarching conclusion that emerges from this effort, it is that, contrary to the notion that capitalism has been transcended, long prevailing imperatives of a market economy remain as determining as ever in the transformations occurring in the technological and informational spheres.

The new communication technologies that have been discovered, the mode of their invention, the processes by which they have been installed, the factors which determine their utilization, the products that have been forthcoming, and the beneficiaries of the new systems and means of information transfer, are phenomena understandable best in terms of long-established and familiar market-based criteria.

Easily discoverable are such old standbys as state subsidies to private undertakings: risk avoidance while insisting on special premiums for risk-taking; competition between capitals at national and international levels; shifting the considerable and never calculated costs of the new productive arrangements to the working population; and, the customary claims of public benefit for what is unabashed private enrichment. Underpinning each of these "principles" of free enterprise, is the promotion of the private accumulation of corporate capital, regardless of the public good or interest.

The elevation of private, corporate over public, social interest is especially transparent in the dynamic communication-information sector. Here the institutional processes are being arranged to, enable the already powerful to seize control and direct the new technologies to corporate ends, while the few public structures with potential countervailing influences are progressively weakened.

In this sector too, the most aggressive elements in American capitalism are the major activist forces. Simon Ramo, director and one of the founders of TRW, Inc., an important electronics company, explains the significance of the information-military connection in the 1980's:

"Our military expenditures will probably increase as a percentage of the GNP over the next decade, and this could be extremely pertinent and beneficial to our leadership position in information technology, especially in computers and communications. This is because the right way for us to enhance our military strength in weapons systems is through superior communication, command, control, and overall utilization of our weapons systems—functions that depend on superior information technology."[1]

That this development occurs in the information-communication sector is particularly grievous. The justification of the new communication technology rests heavily on its promise to reduce inequalities and extend educational, cultural, and human opportunities, locally, and internationally. The institutional arrangements that are being established, however, work toward an altogether different outcome. How does this happen?

A two-century old drama—one that occurred first in the early industrializing process—is being reenacted. Naturally, the participants are different, the social customs altered, the language and metaphor that describe the developments "modern." The actual processes are quite familiar.

Beginning with the discovery process itself, the subsidies go to the super corporations. Once an invention, a process, or facilities are developed and operating—invariably at public expense— they are turned over to private controllers. These then declare that the new enterprise must "pay its own way." The market, totally ignored and by-passed to this point, is now summoned to preside over the new informational capability. It is no surprise that the "someone" who can pay is not coming from the disadvantaged part of the community.

Under the stimulus of market criteria, the new information technologies, for all their exciting features and potential, wind up facilitating the activities and expanding the influence of the already-dominant elements in the social order. At the same time, the practice of treating information as a commodity—an outgrowth

[1]Simon Ramo, *America's Technology Slip*, John Wiley and Sons, New York, 1980, page 283.

of applying market criteria to information—promises to exacerbate old inequities in new ways.

These are the directions manifest in the American economy's information "miracle," now being extended to the world-at-large. The conclusions reached in this work, concerning the new communication technologies and information developments in recent years, derive from an appreciation that American capitalism is still dominant, though challenged, in the world business system.

With this in mind, it is helpful, I believe, to remember that the initial work and analyses in the 1970's on what began to be called the "post-industrial society" and the "information economy," were written at a time, and reflective of a period, when there was still domestic and international economic expansion. Though signs were present, the full dimensions of the world economic crisis were not yet evident. Accordingly, the work at this time continues to take for granted the expansion of social services, widening education for increasing numbers, and an uninterrupted range of benefits issuing from the so-called Welfare State. Indeed, all of these widely-accepted and well-publicized social attributes of advanced capitalism were expected to be strengthened by the new communication technologies that were beginning to appear.

Similar to other widely prevalent views, the thinking then in communications paid little attention to structural features in the newly-emerging information order. It was believed, if not explicitly stated, that *growth* in information supply was the solution for all still-troublesome problems. Illiteracy, educational differentials, political apathy, international tension, cultural pollution and whatever else disturbed the atmosphere, could be overcome with more information.

In the economy-at-large, economists too, welcomed a continuously expanding pool of goods and services. Resource and income inequality could go unattended indefinitely, it was imagined, as long as everyone could get a share, however slight and unequal, of an ever growing national output. In the information-communication community, this thinking expressed itself in endorsing more education, more broadcasting, more media and more information for everyone. Never mind the character, quality, the differentials, and the glut, that in itself posed a major obstacle to understanding. If everyone received more information, it was believed, the course was a correct one.

The stagnation in the world economy in the last few years has changed rapidly and dramatically the context of the discussion. The expectations of increased social services and education, the high but unfounded hopes for the autonomy and social contributions of a "new class" of mind workers are being set aside, if not buried, with few signs of embarrassment.

Wage cuts and freezes, speedup, packaged as "productivity," unemployment, the emergence of a politics using the language of "moderation" at the same time as it is slashing the living standards of the population and financing an almost out-of-control armaments expansion, and the intensification of inter-capitalist rivalries, are the features of the early 1980's, likely to be extended indefinitely.

Mr. Felix Rohatyn, senior partner with the investment banking firm Lazard Freres & Company, and Chairman of the Municipal Assistance Corporation for New York, gloomily sees the current situation this way: "The country's problems are so deep-seated, do-mestically and internationally, economically and socially, that even temporary and partial solutions (and that is probably the best that can be achieved) will, in my view, be beyond any one man, one party, one ideology."[2]

Under these circumstances, the likelihood of gliding into an electronic Utopia becomes at best, an illusionary prospect. But there should be no uncertainty about who occupies the pivotal command places in this crisis-stricken system. Silicon Valley, the heartland of the electronics industry, along with the long-standing owners and directors of the media, the producers and sellers of information systems and products, and the controllers of the communication technology, supply growing numbers of representatives to the political governing process.

The economic role of the information and media industries and the services they provide, are now primary factors in the maintenance of the material system of power, domestically and internationally. It follows that if effective opposition is to develop against the intensifying attacks on the standard of living and against the democratic features of the social order, understanding the realities of electronic information production, dissemination and control in the United States, is imperative.

[2]Felix Rohatyn, "The Older America: Can It Survive?" The *New York Review of Books*, Vol. XXVII, Numbers 21 & 22, January 22, 1981, page 16.

The longer the belief endures that we enjoy a bountiful and benign information system, unstintingly offering us an increased understanding of social reality, and separated by some veil of "social
responsibility"[3] and technological neutrality from the structure of
ownership and decision-making that dominates in all other sectors
of the system, the greater our peril.

As stagnation continues and its effects spread throughout the
economy, a strong eventuality, the actual contours of the "information economy" will become more evident. So too will the interests
and forces that promote and utilize it. Still, it is an obligation to try
to shorten the time for this realization to develop.

For this reason, the issue of *who decides* in this onrushing electronic economy is a matter of vital interest. The great growth of
professional jobs and managerial positions in a few, industrially advanced private ownership economies has been interpreted vari-
ously as foretelling the emergence of a new class, a weakening of
the industrial capitalist ownership class, and, even, as the transcendence of capitalism itself. Yet, attention given to a "new class"
provides a convenient, if essentially lexical way of disposing of the
classes still on the premises—those, whatever their jobs, who work
for others, *and* the "others."

Capital accumulation, and the utilization of the power of the
State for corporate ends are the primary and daily activities, which
constitute late 20th century American social reality. "What is crucial," Victor Ferkiss writes, "is not whether television, computers,
and similar means of communication and control exist and are ab-
sorbing more and more of the material and personnel resources of
all societies, but rather what if anything this has to do with social
structure and economic and political power. Does being an employee of IBM rather than U.S. Steel make any difference in one's
economic or political activities via-à-vis others?"[4]

Bertram Gross, too, informs us, that

". . . in a complex system, the growing importance of some com-
ponent-like radar instruments on an airplane—does not mean it is in
charge. Executive managers are, of course, steering instruments,
are used as such, and are particularly valued to the extent that they

[3]Siebert, Fredrick S., Theodore Peterson, and Wilbur Schramm, *Four Theories of the Press*, Urbana, Illinois, University of Illinois Press, 1956.
[4]Victor Ferkiss, "Daniel Bell's Concept of Post-Industrial Society: Theory, Myth and Ideology," The *Political Science Reviewer*, Vol. IX, Fall 1979, pp. 91–99.

are self-starting, and, subject to vague clues from above, self-steering. Despite some personal stockholdings, the higher executives are "hired executives." Their power and glory derive from service and subservience to superiors—above all, from their ability to provide this service most of the time without explicit tutelage. They can be ruthlessly fired if they fail to accumulate the capital that their overseers deem possible."[5]

I take these arguments to be unexceptional. Attention in this work, therefore, is not on a new class administering the growing flows of information or on speculative scenarios of expanding individual informational autonomy. It is rather on an examination of the structure and operation of the electronic information industries *within the context of the system overall:* how they are organized; who directs them; under what rules they operate; and, how they contribute to, and sometimes influence, the general economy's behavior.

A possible consequence of this emphasis may be that there is an overestimation of the power of the transnational and national business system surveyed. If indeed there is, it occurs partly because of geographical and personal considerations. It is difficult not to be influenced by the very tangible evidences of power and its still relatively uncontested position in the domestic field. Yet it is clear, and I hope evident in the work, that powerful as the position of the United States world business system, and its information industry component in particular, are, they are far from invincible, either from external challenge or internal resistance. A fuller accounting than is presented here of the innumerable sources of opposition, some developed, some latent, would reduce significantly, the image of omnipotence that may inadvertently reveal itself in the analysis.

My admission, that the full dimension of the contradictions and weaknesses that are inherent in the American economy and informational system may have received less than their proper acknowledgement, should not be regarded as another instance of mannered academic apologetics. It is made to alert the reader not to be overcome and consequently paralysed by what may appear to be the emergence of a powerful and unassailable information apparatus, at the disposition of a system of concentrated, corporate capital.

All of the developments that are reviewed in this work are the outcome of complex interactions of economic, political and cultural

[5]Bertram Gross, *Friendly Fascism*, M. Evans & Co., New York, 1980, page 72.

forces. People are either directly or indirectly involved in all of them. The forms the technologies assume are ultimately relations organized for or imposed on people. In the same sense, therefore, people can be determining in the creation of their own technological and informational space *if*, along with the presence of other circumstances facilitating change, they know what their reality actually is.

The succeeding discussions, I hope, will assist somewhat in an understanding of the current and developing information environment that is becoming pervasive wherever corporate capitalism exists or penetrates.

Awesome as the new information technologies are, it is our acceptance that permits them to be utilized and to operate. We possess the power to use or modify them to our own purposes, or, if that is not feasible, to thwart, resist or abandon them. It remains a human decision.

NOTE

Two brief methodological considerations affect the text:

The current pace of technological change and the organizational efforts to cope with and exploit it, according to market norms, create enormous problems of "keeping up" with the data and developments. The flood of legislative actions, corporate, strategic, and financial moves, the outpouring of new products for business and consumer use, to say nothing of the volume of industrial statistics, simply defy immediate categorization and chronicling. For these reasons, some of the data compiled in this study may be out of date by the time of publication. In mitigation of this deficiency, I feel that the *relationships* the current data reveal, the *trends* that are presented, and the *directions* of the developments detailed are not nearly so ephemeral.

Throughout the work, I use the expression *The Fortune 500* as a generic term for the largest corporations in the country. The actual *Fortune 500*, an annual compendium of manufacturing firms, excludes banks, insurance companies, utilities, etc. I intend these to be included in my use of the term.

chapter one

Whose New International Economic and Information Order?

The U.S. leads the world as producer, consumer, processor, and exporter of communication goods and services. Americans preside over the bulk of the channels and the content of the worldwide information flow. American professionals, business men and women, civil servants, educators, and leaders in virtually every field operate increasingly in international frameworks; the same is true of the nation's information and cultural gatekeepers.

Chronicle of International Communication,
January 1980, 1 (1).

Production sites in the world economy are shifting. They are being relocated globally by transnational corporations that seek maximum profits by taking advantage of international differentials in wages, taxes, raw material availabilities, and political complaisance. Simultaneously, a spectacular growth of a new communication technologies facilitate the operations of those companies that carry on their business in dozens of countries.

While this is the reality, a different set of expectations prevailed in much of the world community for at least the last twenty years. These were expressed in the demands for a new world economic and, later, information order. These demands were predicated on the determination of people in the former colonial countries and other dominated areas to shake off the shackles of poverty forged, largely, by economic and cultural dependency.

Yet deep structural changes in the social and productive spheres inside both the dominating and dominated states have always been a precondition for the realization of equal relationships between poor and rich nations and peoples. The full dimensions of a new world economic order, from this perspective, have never been fully articulated. Still, it was clear that most of the prevailing economic assumptions and relations governing production, distribution and, indeed, what constituted "development" itself, were open to review and revision.

The demand for a new world information order—a demand which emerged more slowly—reflected similar impulses. The definition and presentation of everyday reality, nationally and internationally, have been the prerogatives of a score of media conglomerates. The concentrated control of information by Western monopolies has created enormous difficulties for those seeking economic self-determination and political autonomy. By their information selection and control, the Western media, wherever they operate or penetrate, assist in providing the transnational corporate business system with diverted and disoriented domestic publics. Information management for years permitted the dominating centers to ignore or misrepresent the Third World demands for new economic and cultural-informational arrangements.

Now new tendencies can be observed. The far reaching industrial and technological shifts occurring under the inititatives and guidance of transnational business provide an opportunity for—if not necessitate—the centers of domination to adopt the language, if not the substance, of socially desirable change. The new electronic industries, the changing sites of industrial production, and the sophisticated instrumentation that permits high volume, and instantaneous international communication are imposing a new form of hierarchical organization on much of the world.

At the same time, these developments are being described as facilitating a new global economic and informational order. But this is an "order" quite unlike the one perceived originally by the Third World and Non-Aligned Nations. It does not arise out of dependency and the desire to overcome it—the inspiration of the poor world—but derives from the beneficiaries of domination and their intention of perpetuating that domination.

The economic and social transformations now taking place around the world, and the effort to present these changes as the answer to longstanding demands at home and abroad for a substantively new economic and informational order, are the subjects of this chapter.

TRANSFORMATION IN THE WESTERN INDUSTRIALIZED ECONOMIES

What is happening, it is important to state at the outset, is not a linear, preconceived and predetermined transformation of the international political economy. The energizing stimuli heavily influencing what is now occurring are the relatively recent substantive changes in the American economy and in a few other industrially advanced economies. Briefly put, change on a global scale is being activated by a complex set of pressures, initiatives, and requirements arising out of domestic developments in a few core industrial areas, foremost of which is the United States.

A summary review of some of the significant changes in the American economy since the end of the Second World War is suggestive (though it should be noted that the following account accepts unquestioningly descriptions of the American economy as "pluralistic" and controlled by "middle management administration"):

> Consider the shrinking percentage of blue-collar workers in the labor force, with the near-doubling (inflation discounted) of the gross national product since W.W.II; the expansion of research and development in governmental and business budgets and the flowering of major new industries built on the technologies of solid-state electronics and information processing; the transformation of family-owned big business into multinational conglomerates under multilayered middle-management administration; the substantial growth of the not-for-profit private governmental sectors of the pluralistic U.S. economy; the proliferation of the control functions of the Federal Government into many aspects of the economy.[1]

Within the overall pattern, the most striking development is the phenomenal growth of the so-called information sector, a not too clearly defined category that includes the production of information technology and goods and the information services utilized by the rest of American industry (and society). This sector is estimated to have accounted for almost half of the gross national product in 1967, and still more since that time. [2] Though there is increasing skepticism about such calculations, there can be little disagreement about the very rapid growth of information activities in the United States.

New industries have appeared in the last 30 years, producing a spectacular range of electronic instrumentation which, in turn, has been installed rapidly, though unevenly, in manufacturing and services across the country. The productivity of the domestic economy is more and more reliant on information processes and electronic systems. According to one estimate, 30 percent of the labor force is "currently in contact with computers on a daily basis." It is claimed that in the early 1980s the figure will increase to 50 percent and reach 70 percent by 1985. [3] Rarely encountered twenty years ago, computers and microprocessors today are literally household items.

While the domestic importance of computerization grows almost daily, the well-being of the information industries which provide the hardware and services is increasingly dependent on the *world* market for growth and sales. In a magazine forum organized by *Datamation* reviewing the status of the semiconductor industry, two key figures in the field emphasized the importance of the international market for U.S. producing companies. H. Gunther Rudenberg, senior staff member of Arthur D. Little, Inc. observed: "It's an international production scene and an international marketing scene". Roger Bender, president of NEC Microcomputers, added: "Fortunately—or unfortunately, depending on your point of view —the U.S. semiconductor industry is world-oriented; it invests heavily in R & D, and it is not going to roll over and be absorbed by foreign manufacturers."[4]

Information machinery, information services, information products, and information "know how" have become increasingly significant components of American foreign trade, as well as supplying dynamism to the domestic economy. An Arthur D. Little study estimated that the world market for telecommunications equipment would more than double between 1977 and 1987, going from $30 to $65 billion, and with the greatest market potential for the developing nations.[5]

Trade figures for 1979 showed that, in contrast with other sectors of American manufacturing, where exports have been lagging and the nation's overall trade balance is in deficit of more than $30 billion, "U.S. manufactures of computers and business-related equipment scored a trade surplus of more than $4 billion."[6] The surplus was still more substantial in 1980.

Assessing these trends, the Administrator of the National Telecommunication and Information Administration (NTIA), told a congressional subcommittee in March, 1980, that "telecommunications and information merchandise exports [excluding services] represented 10% of the overall U.S. merchandise exports in 1977. Overall, the telecommunications and information sector, together with agriculture and aviation, are currently the leading portions of the export market of the United States."[7]

More significant in the long run is that in services too (the processing and transmission of date), U.S. firms are increasingly active internationally. "U.S. computer firms," one observer notes, "are major world suppliers, deriving about half of their revenues from overseas sales; overseas revenues of U.S. computer firms from sales of services was one billion dollars in 1976 for both on-line and software services and may increase to more than two billion dollars by 1981."[8]

Yet as these information goods and services flow *out* of the country, streams of data flow *in*, are processed, and are returned to the international information current as U.S. products. This interactive flow of information, involving the American and the international economy, is a vital feature of contemporary world market relationships. The United States is "the world's leading importer of data,"[9] at the same time that it dominates the export field.

Another dimension adds additional importance to the information sector. It has been recognized for some time that familiar cultural products and services—film, TV programs, books, news, records, etc.—besides offering entertainment, are ideological items embodying social values and messages and consequently influencing the organization of the entire social enterprise. Yet computerization and data processing, as well, exert a marked, if still unobserved, impact on the social terrain.

Such vital matters as the locus of decision making—the issue of centralization or local control—are affected, if not determined, by the structure and operation of the (imported) electronic telecommu-

FIGURE 1.1
THE NATURE OF TRANSBORDER DATA FLOWS

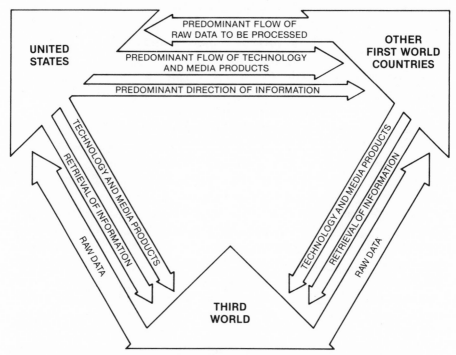

Source: *Transnational Data Report*, March 1980, *2* (8). Originally in AFIPS *Report on Transborder Data Flows.*

nications facilities. So too, questions of the organization of the workplace and labor's role in production are bound up with the information systems now being introduced.

Dominique Wolton of the University of Paris spent several months in the United States, interviewing journalists and publishers about the new communication technologies. He was startled to find that practically no attention was given to the question of the impact of the new systems and instrumentation on the character of the work and the work process itself. He wrote:

> The fact that the transition from paper to computers is bound to modify the process of intellectual creation was never mentioned. Yet the new technology necessarily makes this creative process more abstract, involving an essentially visual, rather than a material or tactile, relationship to writing, which now occurs within the fixed space of the display screen. Who can deny that here we have the seeds of a change in the journalist's relation to his work?

and

> Again, little was said about changes in the organization of this work;
> journalists instead made the point that electronic editing allows
> them greater control over their copy. Yet this advance raises the
> question of what will happen to the line dividing the activities of the
> journalist from those of typesetters and other production workers.
> The question gains urgency as the technical capabilities of the former
> encroach on those of the latter.[10]

Wolton also expressed surprise that no consideration seems to
have been given to what the consequences may be of the substitu-
tion of selective, computerized information on demand for the more
general, overall information customarily supplied by newspapers
and other large circulation organs of information.

For both economic and ideological reasons, therefore, the information industries and their ancillary activities have become vital
determinants of existing and future power relations *within* and *between* nations. In the few industrially advanced market economies
that have moved furthest along the informational path, this relationship does not go unremarked. An official British paper, for example, notes that "It is the view of the United Kingdom that
information processing and handling in all its aspects is now *the* critical technology for advanced industrial countries."[11] A recent
French study likewise states that "data processing has become a
strategic sector in most countries."[12] Concern in Canada is manifest in the conclusions of a Special Government Consultative Committee:

> We conclude our work, therefore, not with another recommendation
> but with an exhortation: with all the force at our command, we urge
> the government of Canada to take immediate action to alert the peo-
> ple of Canada to the perilous position of their collective sovereignty
> that has resulted from the new technologies of telecommunications
> and informatics; and we urge the Government of Canada and the
> governments of the provinces to take immediate action to establish a
> rational structure for telecommunications in Canada as a defence
> against the further loss of sovereignty in all its economic, social, cul-
> tural, and political aspects.[13]

In the United States, consideration of the information industries'
priority and well-being takes place within a still larger context. It
involves nothing less than the maintenance, some would say restoration, of corporate America's global economic power.

Indicative of the tone and urgency of the debate, *Business Week*, in mid-1980, announced the necessity for a "reindustrialization of America."[14] The *New York Times* carried five long articles on essentially the same subject in August and September, and former President Carter, at the end of August 1980, created an Economic Revitalization Board.*

Actually, this is the *public* side of a conflict of views and interests *inside* the corporate community on how to arrest the decline of U.S. economic strength worldwide. Powerful economic groups are affected by the decisions that will be made on capital investment, research and development expenditures, protection of domestic industries, and encouragement for the expansion of high technology industries. In any case, the strategic objective is the same: holding or recapturing markets, and restraining and disciplining the domestic labor force. Whatever the public relations messages to the contrary, profitability and the authority of capital over labor remain the fundamental desiderata.

Cyrus Vance, former Secretary of State, informed a Harvard University Commencement audience in June 1980: "There must be reduced consumption and a higher rate of capital investment; a willingness to shift from obsolete industries instead of propping them up with protectionist trade barriers."[15] Academics recommend 'speedier disinvestment' in 'sunset' industries so that people, money and technology can flow to 'sunrise' industries."[16]

Extending the metaphor, the financial editor of *The New York Times* writes: "There are, to paraphrase Benjamin Disraeli, two economies today: one falling, the other rising; one technologically stagnant or decadent, the other young and brilliant. The task of industrial policy is to help the new to emerge, and fertilize or replace the old."[17]

Uncharacteristically, Congress is not lagging here. In an unpublished report to the U.S. Senate Democratic task force on the economy, "a group of nine Democratic Senators has recommended that Congress create an industrial financing bank to provide capital to high-risk ventures in advanced-technology 'sunrise' industries with promising potential for growth and support."[18]

---

*In January 1981, all seven magazines in the *Time, Inc.* conglomerate for the first time took up a single editorial theme and carried articles on the 'revitalization' of America.

As could have been expected, the leaders and representatives of the information industries anticipated the general debate. As early as 1978, one senior analyst related information to global economic developments, and saw bright prospects for U.S. information producers and transmitters:

> A small but increasingly powerful group of decision-makers—in government as well as in industry—are now coming to believe that an ideal way to relate to the world economy is as an idea and knowledge exporter, based on sophisticated information tools. For example, publications, software, and data can be sold abroad for export revenue, and the knowledge and our natural resources still remain at home—you can sell information over and over again and still have it.[19]

Another voice in the information industry community, speaking perhaps for the "powerful group of decision-makers," is that of John Eger, formerly director of the Nixon Administration's now defunct White House Office of Telecommunications Policy. Eger's view of the American role in the information age takes full account of the sea-change shifts in production underway in the United States and around the world. Eger, along with Vance and other 'internationalists', accepts and, in fact, urges an acceleration in the transformation of the domestic economy, eliminating as quickly as possible older, less profitable manufacturing industries. This he realizes, will require an altogether new set of relationships of the American with the international economy.

In truth, Eger's vision comprehends a massively reorganized division of labor worldwide. In this reorganization, the United States would provide the vital information function. "Since the export of information products and the import of raw information is essential to our growing information economy," he writes, "we must treat these efforts as we would any other important sector of our economy." To be sure, such an approach necessitates difficult decisions—which Eger, and the interests he represents, are fully prepared to recommend:

> If we do proceed to bargain on information flow, we will have to be prepared to make trade concessions in other areas, where our technological advantage is smaller and our labor costs greater. The results could well be a loss of jobs in older domestic industries in exchange for guarantees that our growing information industry will continue to expand.[20]

What these ambitious views appear to reflect are the hopes of some influential Americans to maintain, if not restore, an already badly eroded position of global power. The basis of the newer power role, in this perspective, is the electronic industries and their outputs, the technology of which is derived largely from past and present astronomical expenditures on military and space projects.

The design for a worldwide redistribution of industrial production is, of course, not a unilateral American decision. It takes into account historical factors that have been pushing things in this direction for some time. Manufacturing capacity, especially in basic industrial fields, has developed in many countries outside the North American and Western European centers. Two world wars and innumerable regional conflicts have contributed greatly to this movement; opportunities for the emergence of this enterprise in many less developed locales occurred when the outputs of the major industrialized powers were mobilized and channeled into military production. More important still, the rapid expansion of transnational corporate activity in the last three decades has created a substantial number of manufacturing facilities in the less industrially developed nations.

These innumerable manufacturing enclaves, tributes to the profit seeking quest of the transnationals, have been exporting their outputs in mounting volume into the world market. The outcry of some U.S. industries for 'protection' against these goods is indicative of the heavy weather ahead. Efforts such as those of John Eger to encourage the redeployment of the manufacturing base have to be understood in this overall context.

Actually, significant redeployment already is observable in the core of American industry. In its 25th anniversary compilation of the 500 largest United States *manufacturing* corporations, *Fortune* magazine compares the original of 1955 with the 1980 listing. The changes noted suggest that the new international division of labor is well underway:

> Back in 1955, for example, the list was heavily weighted toward such 'basic' industries as metal manufacturing, rubber, food, textiles, autos, and oil. Leaving aside oil, which has to be treated as a special case, companies in these basic industries filled 185 slots on the 500 and accounted for 43 percent of the 500's total sales. Over the years, however, the basic-industry contingent has been losing position. It is

represented now by only 148 companies which account for only 30 percent of the 500's total sales.

In this same 25-year interval, there is another distinctive trend. The high-technology companies have made some of the most conspicuous gains in sales . . .e.g., Xerox (No. 150), and Polaroid (No. 228) . . . .Five of the computer companies in this year's listing—Control Data (which ranks 159), Digital Equipment (No. 187), Memorex (No. 346), Data General (No. 441), and Storage Technology (No. 457)—are among the thirty companies on this year's list *that didn't even exist when the first 500 was put together.*[21]

THE RATIONALE OF COMPARATIVE ADVANTAGE

The public rationale for the suggested redistribution of industrial manufacturing worldwide rests heavily on a doctrine developed in the 19th century: the theory of comparative advantage. It argues that optimum benefits occur when each nation exchanges what it produces most advantageously, i.e., at lowest cost. The doctrine contains more than a little but something less than the whole truth. Most disturbingly, it accepts as fixed conditions of differential capacity or advantage, ignoring the historical factors that may have contributed to the present relationship. The doctrine in this way presents itself as timeless, universal truth, permitting of no change in the underlying conditions and relationships of those caught up in its operation.[22] Comparative advantage is an ideal doctrine, therefore, with which to justify the economic shifts that are occurring today. These are made to appear 'natural', 'inevitable', beneficial, and progressive. Arguments on their behalf circulate widely. The transnational media see to that.

Applying the comparative advantage principle to international data communication—a subject of the greatest interest and concern to the transnational corporations—two enthusiasts describe how benefits are supposed to derive from the doctrine's application:

> In societies in which information activities generate up to half of the GNP, substantial gains in productivity will arise from efficiency gains in that sector. Thus there is good economic reason to use the cheapest, fastest, most accurate, and most complete information facilities available, wherever they may be located. Just as international trade in physical commodities has raised living standards in the world community by allowing use of commodities produced in the

most advantageous places, so societies half of whose economic activities consist of information operations will gain mutual advantage
from shared use of information resources, with each nation working
especially at activities in which it has a comparative advantage. Energy and other scarce resources can be saved by linking distributed
activities electronically, rather than duplicating expensive facilities
in many physical locations."[23]

Actually, this near eulogistic tribute to comparative advantage is
addressed to the developed market economies in Western
Europe—the OECD countries. Since it is these industrialized economies which at this time are challenging the "advantage" of United
States-based information industries and threatening to limit their
operation in Europe, the study from which this passage has been
taken was written to demonstrate the utility of comparative advantage in the field of information to advanced industrial nations. It is
supposed to convince these countries that their interests are well
served if their processing requirements continue to be handled by
American data processing firms.

However, the lesson is there for the less industrialized states as
well. This is the thrust of a comment on the same subject by an executive of an American computer services company:

> Many countries have and are expending efforts to develop compe-
> tence in producing computer and telecommunications hards ware
> and general purpose software with varying degree of success. No
> matter how this works out over time for each country, it is clear that
> a wide variety of very good general purpose equipment and software
> is readily available within all countries at relatively competitive
> prices today. This is likely to be even more true in the future. *So the
> question must be raised as to how much strategic value there really
> is for a country to produce such general purpose hardware and
> software. Are there perhaps other things which have greater strategic
> value to any country?*[24]

The modern proponents of comparative advantage are uniformly
silent about the appalling inequities and dependencies that historically have acompanied the doctrine's implementation. Indeed, the
early post-World War II efforts by Third World countries to overcome economic backwardness and dependency were directed
largely at the effects of comparative advantage as they had accumulated in Asia, Africa, and Latin America. It is a bitter irony that the
exploited countries, some of which are now embarked on at least

limited industrialization, are again being pushed into unequal economic and informational relationships under the guise of comparative advantage.

It should be understood that the shifts, proposed and actual, in the world division of labor, based on an ever-increasing utilization of information in the productive process as well as in the continuously expanding service industries, do not imply a fully developed plan with each participant neatly and consciously assigned a particular slot in the global economy of the future. It is rather, a projection of some developments that have taken place already and other tendencies that are now observable. It is not, therefore, predestined, but it may be predictable. Daniel Bell writes about this:

> Because of a combination of market and political forces, a new international division of labor is taking place in the world economy. . . .It is likely that in the next decades traditional, routinized manufacturing, such as textile, shipbuilding, steel, shoe, and small consumer appliances industries, will be centered in this new tier (e.g., Brazil, Mexico, South Korea, Taiwan, Singapore, Algeria, Nigeria) that is beginning to industrialize rapidly.

Bell believes that this global realignment in production will not be achieved easily or smoothly:

> The response of the advanced industrial countries will be either protectionism and the disruption of the world economy or the development of a 'comparative advantage' in, essentially, the electronic and advanced technological and science-based industries that are the feature of post-industrial society. How this development takes place will be a major issue of economic and social policy for the nations of the world in the next decade.[25]

Bell does not discuss why this largescale shift in worldwide productive activity may be expected to be troublesome. But the nub of the problem is who will shoulder the burden of this vast realignment of productive effort. The answer is, of course, working people. The changing division of labor internationally is being initiated, guided, and implemented largely by the transnational corporate system. It is not, at this time, influenced in the slightest by social need or any larger public interest.

It is the transnational corporation and its unending search for new markets, raw materials, and maximum profitability that is the engine powering the international transformation now proceeding.

Consequently, it is also the chief beneficiary of the changes now occurring, though here too, there are no long term guarantees.

The worldwide media system, for the most part also under transnational control, ignores or misrepresents what is transpiring. When the shift is discussed at all, it is described as historically progressive, a step toward 'modernization', and in the interest of people everywhere, especially those in the poor lands.*

The costs and the burdens—most of which are still to be experienced—are overlooked and unmentioned. An elemental lesson in capitalistic enterprise is being played out on a world stage. Benefits are going to the holders of capital. Burdens are being borne by the vast majority without property stakes.

And so, hard as it may be to accept, for the time being the transnational corporate system has captured, or at least diverted, the movements toward a new international economic and informational order. Both of these movements, the economic and the informational, originated with the impoverished peoples of the world. More than a hundred industrially weak and exploited nations sought, since the Second World War, to create a new international

*Peter Drucker, an astute observer of corporate behavior, uses the comfortable expression "production sharing" to describe this process. "Manufacturing work," he writes, "that is highly labor-intensive will increasingly have to be moved where the labor supply is—that is to the developing countries." Peter F. Drucker, *The Age of Discontinuity*, Preface to the paper edition. New York: Harper, 1978, p.xix.

In the real world of the transnationals, "production sharing" looks somewhat different from Drucker's description. The *New York Times* gives this account of world components produced for U.S. cars: "It's all part of a trend in world industry, with the large indus trial companies concentrating more and more on high technology, research, design and management, and less developed countries beginning to acquire skills in manufacturing goods, including automobile parts, that they can make cheaper and perhaps even better. South Korea and Taiwan, for example provide everything from ignition wires to intake valves, while Brazil manufactures entire auto and truck engines." Edwin McDowell, "Made in U.S.A.—with foreign parts," The *New York Times*, November 9, 1980.

Then there is the "production sharing" that Barbara Ehrenreich and Annette Fuentes describe. In Mexico, Taiwan, South Korea, the Phillipines, Malaysia, and many other Third World countries, millions of young women are being hired by the transnational companies to perform demanding, labor intensive tasks. The human costs of "life on the global assembly line" do not appear on the glossy balance sheets of the new international division of labor. Barbara Ehrenreich and Annette Fuentes, "Life on the global assembly line," *Ms*, January 1981, *9* (7), pp. 53–59, 71.

enviroment in which the economic, political, and cultural fetters that prevented their autonomous development would be broken. Now both movements are seemingly being incorporated into vehicles for facilitating the global relocation and private corporate control of economic activity.

Under transnational corporate direction, production in conventional industrial goods and services is being transferred world wide to sites with impoverished workers, tax exemptions, and complaisant governments.* Information industries are, at the same time, taking over as the central foci of economic activity in the earlier industrialized core areas. As this international relocational process unfolds, the new international economic order is itself recast but hardly into a progressive arrangement.

The new, industrial producer nations are being brought into the existing world structure, carrying on their newly developed industrial activities under market rules and with market criteria that date back at least a century and a half. A United Nations resolution, adopted in 1975, explains and validates the overall process:

> Developed countries should facilitate the development of new policies and strengthen existing policies, including labour market policies, which would encourage the redeployment of their industries which are less competitive internationally to developing countries, thus leading to structural adjustments in the former and a higher degree of utilization of natural resources in the later.[26]

One writer sees the international division of labor resulting from what he terms this "integrative approach" as leading to a familiar condition:

> The main directionality of the linkages in this division of labor—and the international system of which it is a part—is thus such that the developed countries provide the consumption patterns, technology, skills, capital, etc. to the developing countries which then establish production facilities to service the markets of the North.

All of this leads to the bleak conclusion that the *new*, new international economic order "with its reliance on TNEs [transnational

---

*A counter movement could develop with the widespread introduction of microprocessors to all aspects of mass production. Then it may be possible for high technology centers to re-engage in industrial production without any significant labor costs. Few workers will be employed.

enterprises] is not likely to be a framework for a new and more eq-
uitable world economic order but rather designed to stabilize the
present order and thus contain a further deterioration of the developing countries."[27]

The new international *information* order falls neatly into this
general context. As information is crucial for the operation of the
transnational corporate system, there is every reason to expand international communications. Increased linkages, broadened flows
of information and data, and above all, installation of new communication technology, are expected to serve nicely the world business
system's requirements. That they can be considered as constituting
a new international information order is so much additional icing on
the cake of the transnationals.

OPERATIONALIZING THE NEW COMMUNICATIONS TECHNOLOGY IN THE NEW ORDER

Technology plays a vital role in the emerging new scheme of
things. It serves dually: first, to integrate the transnational corporate system, and second, to deepen the dependence of the peripheral world on hardware, software, training, and administration
supplied by that system.

The less developed nations are not to be denied the new technology. On the contrary, technology is being pressed on the poorer
countries in an atmosphere of urgency. "We must offer to expand
communication systems abroad," urges one promoter of U.S. information policy. "Imaginative use of our satellites and earth stations,
shared time on our broadcasting channels, crash projects to produce cheap newsprint—all and more are readily possible."[28]

Technology's role in the less-developed economies will be extended, but under the auspices of the transnational corporate system. This, it is reasonable to be believe, is intended to assure the
implantation of Western developmental models—of production, administration, consumption, and education. Though it is not likely
that the *most* sophisticated instrumentation and processes of advanced capitalism will be made available to the peripheral world,
even in those cases where it is offered the effects will be the
same—dependency, and development patterned on the market
model. Writing about the possible transfer of information technology, one observer notes:

Even if the U.S. Government did subsidize access to U.S. data banks and 'information resources' [the U.S. proposal at the UNESCO 1978 Paris meeting and elsewhere], it is questionable how useful this information would be . . . . In order for information to have real utility it has to be tailored to the needs and circumstances of the user, and this simply is not achieved through the installation of an international data network. However, once the technical, financial, and management skills and infrastructures have been developed, as in the case of Taiwan, Hong Kong, Malaysia and others, then the export of information is related to the export of capability and 'comparative advantage.'[29]

The important consideration at this time, from the perspective of the transnational corporate policymakers, is to get advanced communications technology installed in as many places as quickly as possible. The effort to put the technical infrastructure in place—termed "operationalism" [30]—is as agreeable to the American information industry complex as it is to the transnational system overall.

Suggestive of the efforts undertaken to create an international atmosphere of encouragement, if not urgency, for the rapid adoption of new communications technology, the International Telecommunications Union (ITU) organized a forum in Geneva in September 1979, the introductory section of which was called Telecommunication Perspectives and Economic Implications. The subjects under discussion were: "strategies for dealing with evolving international telecommunications; industrial products and transfer of technology for effective operation; telecommunication services and networks; [and] financing of telecommunications."

Offering views on these important questions was a panel of speakers recruited almost exclusively from the most powerful companies producing equipment in the transnational corporate system. Among them were: the president of RCA, the Vice-President and Chief Scientist of IBM, the President of Siemens AG, the Vice-President of the Executive Board at Philips; the Executive Vice-President of A.T.&T; the Vice President and Group Executive of Hughes Aircraft, and similar ranking officers from Thomson-CSF, NASA, Comsat, and Ericsson (Sweden). Supplying the new instrumentation and processes means consolidating Western long term control in international markets over equipment, replacement parts, servicing, and finance.

"Operationalism," consequently, makes little attempt to ascertain the appropriateness of the items sold or to develop norms for such an evaluation. Useful or not, needed or not, Western suppliers push their wares come what may. Mild attempts to establish international specifications and protective standards are rebuffed and labelled "premature."[31]

INFORMATION INEQUALITY IN THE CENTER OF THE SYSTEM

Though this is small consolation to the rest of the world, in the global shift of economic and informational activity now proceeding *the center of the system, no less than the periphery, experiences deepening inequalities.*

To the developing nations, the new communications technology is promoted as a means of lessening social gaps in education and literacy and as a means of leapfrogging into the modern age, with classrooms and businesses informed from satellite broadcasts. For the already industrialized countries, the promise is of electronically induced democracy, plebiscites, and polls, carried out at home by the touch of a button on the living room TV console.

These are claims the transnational corporate system circulates through its transnational media circuits. Actual developments, in the United States and elsewhere, present another reality. Consistent with market practice, the advantages and capability of using the new instrumentation vary directly with technical and financial ability (to pay). It requires little imagination to guess who benefits from the new information technology in corporation-dominated America, where a few hundred businesses control more that three-fifths of the national economy.

In the very heart of the most advanced 'information society' it is predicted that, contrary to widely publicized claims, the introduction of electronic information systems will deepen information inequality in the social order.[32] And if this is the prospect for a nation with an abundance of informational circuits, what may be expected to occur in those numerous countries where scarcity, weakness, and dependency are still the prevailing characteristics?

THE FREE FLOW OF INFORMATION

In the period from 1940 to 1970, 'the free flow of information' was a major element in United States information and foreign policy.[33] In this earlier time, the objectives generally were limited to the market needs of the American media industries—the news agencies, film and TV-program export sectors, advertising, publishing, and record industries. The doctrine also was directed against the socialist nations, intended to put pressure on them to open up and be susceptible to consumerist ideology.

Though these aims remain important objectives, the information issue, and the free flow of information doctrine in particular, now transcend the somewhat parochial question of expanded markets for American media interests. Information gathering, processing and transmission, have become essential and determining elements in affecting corporate America's position in a new international economic order. William Colby, former director of the Central Intelligence Agency, puts it this way:

> Today the world is facing a choice between free trade and protectionism in international information exchange. As we learned in the field of commmodities, it will be important to choose the path toward freedom rather than protectionism . . . .In the information industry, whether hardware, software, or the rapidly growing field of substantive analysis, a similar strategy for free international exchange must be developed. The benefits of free exchange and the cost of attempts to obstruct it must be articulated.[34]

Just how important the free flow of information doctrine has become to the transnational corporate system's maintenance and survival is noted by another communications analyst. It is, Clippenger writes, "the pillar not only of U.S. civil liberties and individual freedom, but the market economy as well . . . .And many U.S. commentators and officials have avowed that the concept of free flow is a wholly non-negotiable item."[35] If supremacy in the information sector cannot be maintained, American power could shrink to continental confines. The capability to monitor and police the world, for the protection of the corporate system, is also at stake. Former President Carter alluded to this capacity in discussing the SALT II Treaty with Congress:

> As I have said many times, SALT II is not based on trust. Compliance will be assured by our own nation's means of verification, including extremely sophisticated satellites, powerful electronic systems, and a vast intelligence network.[36]

Similarly, the Director of Security Programs for *IBM*—the corporate empire of computing capability—mentions circumspectly the communication functions vital to the survival of the worldwide American business system:

> I believe the paramount objective should be the preservation of the free flow of information across and within national borders balanced by considerations for privacy and national security. This must be the single most important objective simply because of the immense economic and political impact of free information flow in today's society. So much of this information flow takes place beneath the surface of our conscious activities that we literally take it for granted. Perhaps we would only realize its true value and impact if it were restricted.[37]

But historically and currently, the free flow of information is a myth. Selectors and controllers continue, as they always have, to sift and shape the messages that circulate in society. It is always a matter of who the selectors are and whom they represent. And this is an area of which social class is in control.

The free flow of information, as a phrase, does describe well, however, what now occurs in the global information infrastructures that link the transnational business system. In these *privately* organized circuits, the flow *does* move freely between corporate affiliates in the international sphere. Public scrutiny is avoided and strong efforts are made to keep matters as they are.*

But the *Fortune 500* companies are not necessarily limited to transmitting data wthin their corporate structures. As new tech-

---

*Some indication of the intra-transnational corporate information flow internationally is provided by Hewlett-Packard, a major U.S. manufacturing company: "Hewlett-Packard manufactures more than 4000 products for wide-ranging markets which are primarily in manufacturing-related industries. We have 38 manufacturing facilities and 172 sales and service offices around the world, and together these employ about 45,000 people. We have experienced a very rapid growth of about 20% per year, culminating in sales of $1.7 billion in 1978. . . . To support this business, we currently have some 1,400 computers (not including desktop units or handheld calculators). Of these, 85% are used to support engineering and production applications, are usually dedicated to specific tasks, and often are arranged in networks. A number of them are also used in computer-aided design applications as front-end processors for large mainframes. The remaining 200 computers are used to support business applications. . The network tying all this together consists of 110 data communications facilities located at sales and service offices, at manufacturing plants, and at corporate offices in Northern California and Switzerland." (Cort Vån Rensselaer, "Centralize? Decentralize? Distribute?," *Datamation*, April 1979, *25* (4), p. 90).

nology makes all communications processes increasingly interchangeable—i.e., messages, whatever the form, be it record, voice or visual—are reducible to electric impulses. Transnational businesses have the opportunity to reach large audiences and publics on their own terms, possibly through their own informational circuits. (See Chap. 4)

A recent study notes: "The ability to communicate with masses of people is spreading beyond the 'institutional media'."And a United States Supreme Court decision in 1978 approved the principle that "a telephone company, or any other corporation, has First Amendment rights."[38]

In recent years, United States policy makers defended American broadcasters' rights to use direct satellite broadcasting—when it became available—without complying with national oversight from any country. The argument advanced claimed that the world itself was covered by the U.S. Constitution. Now, apparently expanding on that modest interpretation, the international community may be informed that not only American media but *all* U.S. transnational corporations have unlimited global communication rights because they are shielded by the U.S. Bill of Rights.[39]

RECAPITULATION AND FUTURE FOCUS

Industrial competitive pressures, technological developments, social movements, and national policies are changing the contours of the international economy and the global informational system. The change itself is not an issue. It is an ever-present historical phenomenon. What is of concern are the forces that are pushing and directing the current global shifts.

To date, the main activators and controllers of these changes have been the transnational corporations. In responding to their own profit imperatives, economic activity, political behavior, and the cultural environment in much of the world have been affected dramatically. Though the TNCs are not the exclusive agents in determining the mix of production, the character of consumption, the social values attendant on both, and the informational messages circulating worldwide, they are the most influential. This is so because they are the richest and most powerful actors on the international stage at this time.

Given this strength, can the new international division of labor—with informational activity at its apex—be effected according to the design of the transnational corporate system? To begin to answer this question, which concerns a good part of the world economy, the changing structure and character of the American economy—still the center of the world system—must be examined. Following this, the impact of these changes on the international system must be considered. It is to a review of these subjects that the subsequent chapters are devoted.

Notes to Chapter One

1. Eli Ginzberg, "The professionalization of the U.S. labor force,"*Scientific American*, March 1979, *240* (3), p 48.
2. M. U. Porat, "Global implications of the information society,"*Journal of Communication*, Winter 1978, *28* (1), pp.70–80.
3. E. Drake Lundell, "Greater penetration viewed as Critical DP issue,"*Computerworld*, February 19, 1979.
4. "The chip revolution . . . a candid conversation," *Datamation*, June 1979, *25* (7), pp.98–100.
5. *Computerworld*, April 1, 1979, p. 80.
6. *Computerworld*, March 31, 1980.
7. *Transnational Data Report*, May 1980, *3* (1) p.7.
8. W. Fishman, "International data flow:Personal privacy and other matters,"paper presented to the Fourth International Conference on Computer Communication, Kyoto, Japan, February 3, 1978.
9. Angeline Pantages & G. Russell Pipe, "A new headache for international DP," *Datamation*, June 1977, p.115.
10. Dominique Wolton, "Do you love your VDT?," *Columbia Journalism Review*, July/August 1979, 18 (2), pp. 36–39.
11. "Taking a stand on a critical technology,"editorial, *Computing*, September 7, 1978, London, emphasis in the original.
12. Simon Nora & Alain Minc, *L'Informatisation de la Société*, La Documentation Francaise, Paris, 1978.
13. *Telecommunications and Canada*,report of the Consultative Committee of the Implications of Telecommunications for Canadian Sovereignty (The Clyne Report), Ottawa, March 1979, p. 76.
14. *Business Week*, June 30, 1980, cover page.
15. *The New York Times*, June 6, 1980, A 12.
16. Edward Cowan, Books of the *Times*, review of the *Zero-sum society*,by Lester C. Thurow, *The New York Times*, July 1, 1980.

17.   *The New York Times*, June 27, 1980, D2.

18.   Edward Cowan, "Aid urged to 'Sunrise' industries,"*The New York Times*, September 1, 1980, D1.

19.   Vincent E. Guiliano, "Electronic office information systems and the information manager,"*Bulletin of the American Society for Information Science,*February 1978, *4* (3), p.13.

20.   John M. Eger, "Protest of global 'information war' poses biggest threat to U.S.," The *Washington Post*, January 15, 1978.

21.   Linda Snyder Hayes, "Twenty-five years of change in the *Fortune 500*,"*Fortune*, May 5, 1980, pp.90–92, emphasis added.

22.   Wallerstein points out that the advocacy and implementation of the principle of comparative advantage and its complementary doctrine of free trade historically are linked to hegemonic power. If hegemony is defined as a situation in which a single core power has demonstrable advantages of efficiency *simultaneously* in production, commerce and finance, it follows that a maximally free market would be likely to ensure maximal profit to the enterprises located in such a hegemonic power.

"It is no accident therefore that, at the moment of Dutch accession to hegemony in the seventeenth century, Hugo Grotius published that 'classic' of international law, *Mare Liberum*, in which he argued that 'every nation is free to travel to every other nation, and to trade with it', because 'the act of exchange is a completion of independence which Nature requires', (Grotius, 1916). This ideology was revived under British auspices in the mid-nineteenth century and American auspices in the mid-twentieth. In each case, the ideology was practical only to the extent—and as long as—the core power who promulgated it was truly hegemonic."

Immanuel Wallerstein, "World networks and the politics of the world economy," in Amos H. Hawley, Ed.,*Societal growth process and implications,*, New York: The Free Press, 1979, p.273, emphasis in original.

23.   Ithiel de Sola Pool & Richard J. Solomon, "Transborder data flows: Requirements for international co-operation," Organization for Economic Co-operation and Development (OECD), Working Party on Information, Computer and Communications Policy, DSTI/ICCP/78.21, Paris, July 26, 1978, pp.17–18.

24.   Alden Heintz, Vice-President, International and Corporation Operations, Tymshare, Inc., "The computer services industry," in *Data regulations: European and third world realities.*Uxbridge, England: Online, 1978, p. 165, emphasis added.

25.   Daniel Bell, "Communications technology—for better or worse,"*Harvard Business Review*, May-June 1979,*57*(3) p.26.

26.   "Development and international economic cooperation", Resolu-

tion 3362, S-VIII, UN General Assembly, Seventh Special Session, September 16, 1975.

27.   Karl P. Sauvant, "The role of transnational enterprise in the establishment of the new international economic order: A critical review,"Ervin Laszlo & Jorge Alberto Lozoya, Ed., *Strategies for the NIEO*, Oxford: Pergamon, March 12, 1979, p.24.

28.   Leonard R. Sussman, "A new world information order?" *Freedom at Issue*, November/December 1978 (48) p.9.

29.   John H. Clippenger, "The hidden agenda,"*Journal of Communication*, Winter 1979, *29* (1), pp. 189–190.

30.   Benno Signitzer, *Regulation of direct broadcasting from satellites: The UN involvement*. New York; Praeger, 1976.

31.   The U.S. delegate to the Strategies and Policies for Informatics (SPIN) meeting in Torremolinos, Spain, August 1978, stated this explicitly.

32.   Herbert S. Dordick, Helen G. Bradley, Burt Nanus & Thomas H. Martin, "The emerging network marketplace," F35, December 1978. Center for Futures Research, Graduate School of Business Administration, University of Southern California, Los Angeles, CA 90007.

33.   Herbert I. Schiller, *Communication and cultural domination*, M.E. Sharpe, White Plains, N.Y.: 1976, Chap. 2.

34.   William E. Colby, "International information—free trade or protectionism," International Conference on Transnational Data Flows, Washington, D.C., December 3, 1979.

35.   John H. Clippenger, *op. cit.*, p. 199.

36.   *The New York Times*, June 19, 1979, p. A-13.

37.   Harry B. DeMaio, "Transnational information flow: A perspective,"*Data Regulation: European and Third World Realities.*Uxbridge, England: Online, 1978, p.170.

38.   William H. Read, "The first amendment meets the second revolution,"Working Papers, W-79-3. Harvard University Program on Information Resources Policy, Cambridge, Massachusetts, March 1979, pp.25–26.

39.   A Canadian Government study sees this as an imminent reality. "Few people in Canada are aware of the implications of what is happening. These are some of the dangers foreseen if protective measures are not urgently devised and implemented. Greater use of foreign, mainly U.S., computing services and growing dependence on them will . . .facilitate the attempts of the government of the United States to make laws applicable outside U.S. territory." *Telecommunications and Canada* (The Clyne Report), *op. cit.*, p.64.

chapter two

The Infrastructure of the "Information Society"

If there are social benefits to our nation, as we have always believed, in pluralism, in diversity, in lively competition in the marketplace, and in the rights of the individual to maximum freedom of choice within the limits of the social contract, and above all to maximum freedom of speech, then this increasing concentration of corporate power in the most sensitive area in a democracy—the area of communication from one human being to another, from leaders to citizens and vice versa—should surely be a matter of greatest concern.

John Hersey, Final Report of the National Commission on New Technological Uses of Copyrighted Works, July 31, 1978, Washington, D.C., p. 90.

What is called the "information society" is, in fact, the production, processing, and transmission of a very large amount of data about all sorts of matters—individual and national, social and commercial, economic and military. Most of the data are produced to meet very specific needs of super-corporations, national governmental bureaucracies, and the military establishments of the advanced industrial state.

New technology, new industries, new products and new services have come into being which derive profit from these data and which assist, as well, in their production and circulation. Already, institutional patterns have developed to facilitate these many activities. An examination of the communication structures, processes, and relationships currently in place may help to put in perspective the larger forces now at work in advanced capitalist society.

In attempting such an examination, it must be admitted at the outset that the complexity of the new information technology is beyond simple exposition. Many of the developments are difficult to ascertain because of the private nature of most of the arrangements and the technical sheath that conceals many of the socioeconomic factors. Additionally, the field is new, changing rapidly, and has not yet congealed into hard and fast relationships—though, as will be evident, this does seem to be occurring relatively quickly. For these reasons, what follows must be regarded as far from comprehensive. It is intended to be exploratory, suggestive, and certainly not definitive. It is hoped that one issue will remain central throughout all the discussion that follows. This is: How is the information dependency that now afflicts peoples and nations likely to be affected with the advent of the new instrumentation and its control mechanisms?

A few cautionary words are in order at the beginning about the contours of the new information scene. Merely to organize the rapidly proliferating information activities into a few general and readily understandable categories is no easy task. Doing so probably omits and distorts many significant sub-set operational fields. Yet at the risk of such error, this is precisely the approach undertaken in this work. It is done in the belief that a partial representation of reality is preferable to no presentation at all.

Accordingly, three very broad fields of current communication activity are reviewed briefly: hardware, software, and transmission (which is, in some respects, also hardware). Under hardware the main breakdowns are the big (mainframe) computer, the minicomputer, and the semiconductor (integrated circuits) industries. Software includes the computer programs, the data bases, and the data processing and computer services industries. Finally, transmission, in this discussion, signifies the networks, public and private, that have been and are being organized to move the data that have been generated and processed. These three divisions are by no means separate and self-contained. They overlap, and often the same firms and public entities are engaged in all these sectors of communication activity.

HARDWARE

The Main Frame Computer Industry

The singular institutional attribute of the new communication technology, and especially of the big computers, is that almost all the hardware is produced by a very small number of companies. There is one corporation that dominates domestically and internationally.* One account describes this condition:

Watching the movements made by companies and governments in the industry worldwide is like watching 15 chess matches going on at the same time. Every match has one thing in common though. IBM seems to control both queens on every board.[1]

Or, as the *un*authorized biographer of IBM writes: "IBM is not just a major international company in the area of computing, it is the international environment."[2] Currently, IBM operates 44 plants in 15 countries. In 1979, it received about half of its revenues from business outside the United States. In most of the major, developed countries in the world, its share of the communication markets starts at 50 percent.[3] In 1978, IBM had 53.8 percent of Western Europe's market for general purpose computers and nearly 60 percent of the West German market.[4]

IBM also constitutes the domestic computational environment. In 1979, "IBM shipped 65.5 percent of the general-purpose computers and their related peripherals—a market share that in any other industry would be considered startling." As several smaller firms produce equipment that ties into IBM's offering, "one finds that IBM's decisions affect 74.5 percent of the nations's users . . . .To borrow a line from E. F. Hutton [the stockbrokerage firm]—when IBM speaks, *everybody* listens."[5]

Actually, they do more than listen. They often disappear. In 1979, *Itel* Corporation "become another victim of IBM's entrenched position in the marketplace." It joined four other firms forced out of

---

*It is a mark of IBM's standing in the national economy that the Carter Administration contained nine persons with IBM connections in high-ranking positions. Three IBM board directors were in the cabinet. (*Computerworld*, June 25th and October 15, 1979). In the Reagan Administration, IBM promises to be at least as well represented. *Computerworld*(November 10, 1980) noted that "The IBM board in fact has almost served as a 'mini government in waiting' between elections.'"

FIGURE 2.1
THIS FIGURE PRESENTS IBM'S SHARE OF THE UNITED STATES
MARKET FOR GENERAL-PURPOSE COMPUTERS IN A RECENT YEAR.

THE MAINFRAME COMPUTER MARKET
Share of mainframe market based on
the value of total units installed

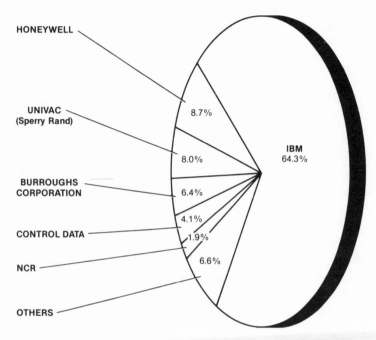

HONEYWELL

UNIVAC
(Sperry Rand)

8.7%

IBM
64.3%

8.0%

BURROUGHS
CORPORATION

6.4%

4.1%

CONTROL DATA

1.9%

6.6%

NCR

OTHERS

Source: *Quantum Science Corporation*
Copyright: 1979/1980 by the *New York Times Company*. Reprinted by permission.

the business in the last ten years, "and all have left primarily because of IBM's dominance in that market."[6]

The size of the market for computers already is impressive. Its
near term potential, projecting current installation trends, suggest
that computers will constitute one of the world's largest industries.
The power these developments confer on a corporation that now
dominates the field, therefore, can hardly be overestimated. The
current situation and the short term trends are shown in Table 2.1.

Minicomputers

Home run hitters and touchdown makers get the most attention
and so it is with the big, mainframe computer producers. All the

TABLE 2.1:   WORLDWIDE COMPUTER
             INDUSTRY: INSTALLED
             BASES[a] IN $ MILLIONS AT SALES
             VALUE

Country	As of 12/31/75 (in millions $)	As of 12/31/80 (in millions $)
United States	39,750	62,700
Western Europe	22,050	38,800
Other countries (including Japan)	11,600	23,050
	73,400	124,550

[a]Installed base is the value of the equipment in place.
Source: Sperry Rand (*Datamation*, September 1976, p. 57.

same, there are other players in the industry. The mini-computer
sector turns out small, low-cost data processors, and is a booming
field. In 1978, revenues in this area were $3.65 billion, and it is ex-
pected to be a $13 billion market in 1983.[7] There are only a few sig-
nificant producers in this not much more than twenty-year-old
industry, the leader is Digital Equipment Corporation (DEC).
DEC and the other main firms, with their market shares, are presented in Figure 2.2.

How specific market shares in this sector will evolve is difficult to
predict. What is certain is the direction of its evolution. Further
concentration, and consolidation into the domains of a few powerful
businesses already on the scene, is the likely development.

Semiconductor Industry

The integrated circuit or semiconductor industry constitutes a
third and critical sector in the communication hardware category.
Its product, the silicon chip containing miniaturized circuits, is the
basis for the entire electronics industry—a field which "is growing
so fast that [it] could be a $400 billion industry by the late 1980s, a
figure that puts electronics in the same league with oil, automo-
biles, and other giants of the business world."[8] The chip is the basic
element of computers, telecommunications items, pocket calcula-
tors, industrial process control equipment, scientific instruments,
and defense systems.

The semi-conductor industry has received heavy publicity in recent years as an example of dynamic capitalism; it is a field in which

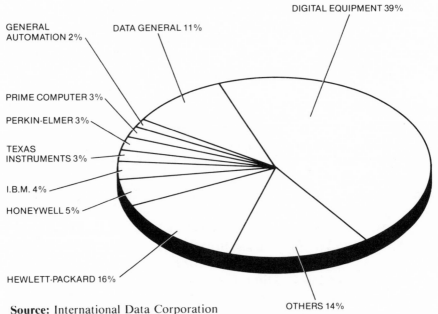

FIGURE 2.2
DIVIDING THE MARKET FOR MINICOMPUTERS
Market share in 1979 based on revenues attributable to minicomputers

DIGITAL EQUIPMENT 39%

GENERAL
AUTOMATION 2%

DATA GENERAL 11%

PRIME COMPUTER 3%

PERKIN-ELMER 3%

TEXAS
INSTRUMENTS 3%

I.B.M. 4%

HONEYWELL 5%

HEWLETT-PACKARD 16%

OTHERS 14%

Source: International Data Corporation
Copyright: 1979/1980 by the *New York Times Company.* Reprinted by permission.

entrepreneurship is alive and flourishing. Business and popular papers have been filled with stories of individuals who have established small research and manufacturing firms which, in a few years, expanded into multimillion (and sometimes hundreds of million) dollar businesses. "Silicon Valley" in northern California has been described as a vision of the future embodying all the virtues of the past: initiative, enterprise, and industrial growth.

Taken out of historical and social context, it does seem as if the semiconductor industry has given a remarkable performance and demonstrated at the same time what capitalism, in its youth, was supposed to be all about: invention, application, risk, rapid growth, and product improvement. Overlooking the large element of myth surrounding what actually happened during capitalist development, capitalism is certainly not now in its youth. The semiconductor industry is better appreciated as a revealing example of late capitalist development. For this industry came into existence on the basis of huge governmental research funds allocated to maintain and expand the American corporate and military global presence. One example of many, "the Minuteman missile program in particular . . . greatly aided the development of integrated circuits by providing a market for the devices when they were just getting off the ground."[9] Military support for the microcircuit industry has by no means abated. The "electronic warfare market," according to *The New York Times*, has grown from $500 million in 1974 to $3.6 billion currently, and is expected to reach $5.7 billion by 1983.[10]

Some individual scientists and engineers were able to seize the opportunities available for private projects financed with federal funds in the lush but brief interval that was once supposed to be the launching of an 'American Century'—circa 1950–65. As the President of the Computer and Business Equipment Manufacturers Association (CBEMA) put it: "In the early days of computer development and application, the government was the progenitor, the prod . . .but 'the impetus was lost' sometime during the early 60's."[11]

The high technology firms that sprouted in this period offered the publicists of American enterprise still another chance to glamorize a system that badly needed restoration. Yet this too has lapsed quickly. As a *Science* article reported: "Great Corporations from Tiny Chips Grow . . . .microelectronics companies are changing in character from small, high-technology ventures of the 1950s and 1960s to large, mature corporations."[12]

They are changing so because the capital required to start a microelectronic company in the current state of the art has jumped from $5 million in the 60s to at least $100 million currently. Further, to keep up with the advancing technology, increasingly expensive equipment is required. As has happened throughout capitalist development, the independents and the smaller firms are disappearing: being pushed out, bought up, or merged. "Microelectronics companies are rapidly disappearing as independent entities," *Science* reports.[13] The pace of consolidation can be appreciated in the run-down, presented in Table 2.2, of acquisitions of U.S. semiconductor firms.

Actually, the semiconductor industry is made up of two kinds of manufacturers: the independents, who are disappearing; and, those companies that are already included as divisions of vertically integrated firms. Examples of this second kind are IBM, TI (Texas Instruments), Motorola, and RCA.

TABLE 2.2:   AQUISITIONS OF U.S. SEMICONDUCTOR
FIRMS EST. 1979 I.C.

U.S. Firm	Sales	Affiliation
1. TI	$680	div. of TI Inc.
2. Motorola	425	div. of Motorola Inc.
3. Intel	400	—
4. National Semiconductor	320	—
5. Fairchild	305	acquired by Schlumberger
6. Signetics	250	acquired by N. V. Philips
7. Advanced Micro Devices	160	owned by Siemens
8. Mostek	155	acquired by United Technologies
9. RCA	145	div. of RCA
10. Harris	100	div. of Harris Corp.
11. American Micro Devices	95	acquired by Robert Bosch GmbH
12. Rockwell Semi	85	div. of Rockwell International
13. General Instrument	80	div. of G.I. Inc.
14. Intersil	75	acquired by Northern Telecom
15. Synertek	50	acquired by Honeywell
16. Analog Devices	40	acquired by Standard Oil
17. Monolithic Memories	35	acquired by Northern Telecom
18. Siliconix	30	acquired by Lucas Industries
19. Solid State Scientific	22	acquired by Adolf Schindling
20. Zilog	15	acquired by Exxon

Sources: *Datamation*, April 1980; *SIA; The New York Times.*

The importance of semiconductors continues to grow, with *Business Week* noting that "virtually every U.S. manufacturer will soon be dependent on this technology,"[14] and the international market for integrated circuits has become a scene of ferocious competition. United States' companies now hold two-thirds of the world market, but this apparently commanding position has been shrinking. It had been 88 percent in the 1960s; the Japanese offensive to take over a large chunk of the market grows more fierce.[15] The current breakdown of world market shares on a national and company basis is seen in Table 2.3.

More attention will be given later to the international market for information goods and services, and the increasing rivalries be-

TABLE 2.3: DIVIDING THE WORLD'S MARKET FOR MICROCHIPS

Share of World Market	United States	European	Japanese
10%+	Texas instruments IBM*		
5% to 10%	National Semiconductor Motorola Intel	Philips	
2% to 5%	Fairchild Camera Western Electric Mostek RCA	Siemens	Hitachi Toshiba N.E.C.
1% to 2%	Hewlett-Packard Harris General Instruments Rockwell I.T.T.	Thomson-C.S.F.	Mitsubishi Fujitsu
Total Share	67%	10%	15%

*Company makes integrated circuits for its own use only.
Source: Philips, *New York Times,* January 29, 1980.

tween the United States, Western European and Japanese market economies. However the world market for semi-conductors may be redivided in the years ahead, one development is assured. The small-scale, independent manufacturer will be gone and the integrated circuit industry will be absorbed into some subdivisions of a few transnational corporations. One of the early innovators in the industry predicted this and claimed that "in the 1980's there may be only about ten firms worldwide that remain as major suppliers of microcircuits."[16]

SOFTWARE AND TRANSMISSIONS

While the hardware side of computer communication is being rationalized and transnationalized, similar developments are occurring in the less observable though no less important software side. This part of the computer communication industry includes the instructions (programs) for organizing, processing, and transmitting the data, as well as the data themselves and the prepared packages of data that are customized to meet individual specifications.

One of the most important categories of software is the data base. Data bases are constructed for many purposes, the most familiar of which is the academic/technical/scientific base. This is a set of data in a specific category or area—chemistry, physics, medicine, education, sociology—which has been stored in some suitably accessible form. The size of a base varies, but it may contain millions of records.

Other data bases are organized for the production, planning, and marketing needs of large, private corporations (for payrolls, raw material flows, property accounting, and customers) and for governmental and private administrative units (social security rolls, credit ratings, police records, and health statistics and information). This type of data base presently accounts for the preponderant utilization of computer communications. However, most of these are unavailable for systematic analysis and review because they are regarded as proprietary. Information searches by computer, already widespread, are likely to become standard tools in much of the scientific community's future research activity, to say nothing of their application to everyday business and government operations. In 1979, for example, it is estimated that 4 million on line searches were undertaken.[17]

As computerized data base searching becomes the dominant mode of information acquisition, nothing less than the widest participation in the creation of the data base would be a prerequisite for meaningful information autonomy, locally, nationally, and internationally. This means the fullest opportunity for the user to know what is and what is not in the data base, the criteria for data selection and classification, and how changes may be introduced.

The French-commissioned Nora/Minc report emphasized this point:

> Information is inseparable from its organization and mode of storage. In the long run, it is not only a question of the advantage that may be conferred by familiarity with such and such a set of data. Knowledge will end up by being shaped, as it always has been, by the available stock of information. Leaving to others—i.e., American data banks—the responsibility for organizing this 'collective memory' while being content to plumb it is to accept a form of cultural alienation. Installing data banks is an imperative of national sovereignty.[18]

Nora and Minc are concerned with the implications for national autonomy when information is secured from external data repositories. There are equally valid reasons for concern with the manner in which the *domestic* "collective memory" is being organized inside the United States.

Paralleling developments in the production and marketing of hardware, the software industry (apart from the totally proprietary intra-company computer systems) is being integrated rapidly into socioeconomic control structures. This follows in part from the considerable costs of assembling information. "Putting [a data base] into operation requires the equivalent of 30 man years of work, an initial cash outlay of $.08 to $1 million and an annual operating expenditure of between $120,000 and $200,000."[19]

In a market economy, the questions of costs and prices inevitably play the most important, if not determining, roles in what kind of base will be constructed and the category of user the base is intended to serve (and by which it is to be paid for). The selection of material that goes into a data base is closely linked to the need for, and the marketability of, the information service. If corporate and government bureaucracies are the intended users—which happens most often because of their needs and ability to pay—their informational requirements will strongly influence the items put into the base, as well as the classifications adopted for easy retrieval of the information.

Currently, for example, financial data base services are largely the province of three Anglo-American corporate subsidiaries. Chase Econometrics (Chase Manhattan Bank), Reuters (English news agency) and AP-Dow Jones "supply most of the world's demand for financial information."[20].

An inventory of the data bases in operation worldwide can only be provisional at this time, as new bases are being created continually both nationally and internationally. For instance, in the last three months of 1979 alone, 50 data bases were offered in the U.S. for the first time, "and one estimate claimed that 450 bases were then available on-line."[21]

In addition, corporate data banks, which comprise the bulk of data bases now in use, must be excluded from this analysis because they are not accessible to the public. Table 2.4 presents information on 528 data bases (exclusive of corporate bases) in operation in

TABLE 2.4: DATA BASES IN OPERATION IN 1979 IN
THE UNITED STATES, CANADA, JAPAN
AND EUROPE (EXCLUSIVE OF
PRIVATE, INTRA-CORPORATE
BASES)[22]

Area	No. of Bases	No. of Records Held	% of Records Held
U.S.	259	93,500,000	63
Non-U.S.	269	54,500,000	37
	528	148,000,000	100

Europe, Canada, Japan and the United States at the end of 1979.
Numerous small bases which had little effect on the general picture
were not included.

With respect to *organized* data—the essential prerequisite for
utilization in an information-based economy—the United States in
1979 was ahead of other industrialized nations; almost two-thirds of
the records held in organized data banks were located in U.S. data
bases. Of these, the U.S. Government accounted for 25 percent and
the private sector for 75 percent. Of that 75 percent, for-profit organizations have 44 percent and the not-for-profit organizations
have 31 percent. (Actually, the not-for-profit component in the private sector may be misleading. Increasingly, the designation "not-
for-profit" is a convenient organizational means to avoid certain
obligations while providing *de facto* commercial opportunities and
benefits to its administrators.

One other characteristic of these existing data bases in the
United States, Canada, Japan and Europe is worth mentioning.
Presented here is the distribution of the bases by category of information held. As shown in Table 2.5, it is striking that the non-
scientific and technical category of information in all the reported
data bases totalled only 5 percent of all U.S. and 3 percent of all
non-U.S. non-corporate records held, whereas science-technology,
science, and technology-related records accounted for 95 percent of
the data held. One European study suggests that this reflects the
development of publicly available computer-based information
services that have been spin-offs from the massive U.S. Government investment in Defence and Aerospace. These government
agencies developed a methodology and technique of information

TABLE 2.5:   DISTRIBUTION OF DATA BASES IN U.S., CANADA, JAPAN AND EUROPE IN 1979 BY CATEGORY OF INFORMATION HELD (EXCLUSIVE OF PRIVATE, INTRA-CORPORATE BASES)[23]

Information Category	U.S.		Non-U.S.	
	% Db	(% Records)	% Db	(% Records)
Science and technology	47	(65)	53	(75)
Mixed	62	(30)	38	(22)
Arts/Humanities	40	(1)	60	(.5)
Soc. Sciences	29	(4)	71	(2.5)
		100.0		100.0

handling to satisfy their own information needs. This methodology, updated to capitalize on advances in computer technology, is used by all the major international information services, such as System Development Corporation (SDC), Lockheed, the Space Documentation Service of the European Space Agency, and, also the major European operations.[24] Moreover, much of the assembled data originated in U.S. military and military-related research and development after World War II. The enormous R&D budgets of the Pentagon, over three decades, have generated a good share of the information that currently resides in the data bases now functioning.

Other developments are occurring that are rapidly transforming the organization and availability of data in the United States. There is, on one side, an uninterrupted assemblage of bases into ever larger aggregations of data available for a price. At the same time, new data base providers are appearing that are markedly different from the first data generators: the academic, scientific, and governmental producers. And, super corporations now are offering data amassed often for their own operations and made available for customized reworking, which they also will provide.

Considering the aggregation of existing data bases first, already a few corporations or corporate subsidiaries have emerged as significant data base organizers and data suppliers. Lockheed, for example, with its DIALOG information and retrieval system, contends that it is "the largest and most extensive collection of on-line [interactive] data bases in the world."[25] In 1980 it offered some

100 different data bases to its customers, including Foreign Trad-
ers Index (FTI), a data base prepared by the U.S. Department of
Commerce's Export Information Division.[26]

The FTI data base "contains information on 150,000 firms in 130
countries, specifically with regard to the firms' contacts for international trading purposes. The file is designed to produce lists of potential foreign contacts for U.S. businessmen and corporate
executives." Of some additional interest, especially to those pro-
fessing attachment to the free flow of information, is that "access to
this file is being restricted to U.S. organizations under terms of
Lockheed's agreement with the Commerce Department."[27]

At the end of 1975, it was estimated that there were 2000
organizational users of on-line search services worldwide, of which
32 percent were commercial, 31 percent educational, 21 percent
government agencies, 10 percent nonprofit, and 6 percent other. Of
the overall total of users, Lockheed claimed that its customers exceeded 1000. or more than half of the worldwide use at that time.[28]
In addition to Lockheed, other U.S. firms—System Development
Corporation; Bibliographic Retrieval Services, Inc.; Mead; and
Informatics—actively promote these services.

The main developments in data organization and supply are now
coming from a new direction. *Fortune 500* corporations are moving
into the field in a massive way. Already possessing sizable computer and data processing facilities, they are selling some of the information they produce for their international operations,also
selling time on their computers and increasingly offering data processing operations to the specifications of interested customers.
These developments allow new sources of profitmaking, assist di-
versification, and assure a place in the emerging arena of information control on a large scale. Thus, *Fortune* reports that "the entire
on-line information industry is currently going through a minor cat-
aclysm of combination and recombination."[29]

Some of the business giants now entering the data processing
and supply field move only a short distance from previous activities. McGraw-Hill Corporation, for example, is regarded still as a
major publisher of books and magazines. Among its holdings are
Standard & Poor's Stock Index, the Dodge construction index,
Platt's Oilgram Price Report, and Data Resources, Inc. These and
other information activities have permitted McGraw-Hill to be-

come "a world leader in the booming business of providing information to industry, goverment, and individuals."[30] The voluminous data flows that supply the many familiar publishing enterprises of the company now are being organized and packaged for electronic distribution.

Another, different kind of entry into the electronic information processing and supply field is exemplified by *Citibank*, the second largest commercial bank in the United States. *Citibank* began to make its considerable in-house computer capacity available to non-banking customers in 1976. Additionally, it has been offering special services to the public such as a credit analysis system, an on-line financial data base, a securities data base, investment and economic planning, software, and related items. These services are being sold in 174 cities in the United States and around the world.[31]

Citibank, a mammoth financial enterprise with "virtually no limit to the potential scope of [its] new burgeoning enterprise,"[32] is not alone in its data supply options. *Exxon*, the largest oil corporation in the world, has also moved into information processing and is expected to have subsidiaries in this field producing $10 to $15 billion in revenues by the end of the 1980s.[33] Still to be taken into account are the enormous resources of the telephone monopoly, A.T.&T., that are being mobilized for entry into the field. Part of the restructuring which is occurring throughout the computer and communication industries involves the imminent appearance of A.T.&.T. as a data processor and distributor, activities hitherto closed off to the Bell empire but now made legitimate under what is euphemistically called "de-regulation."[34]

The tremors from these decisions to enter the information field of the most powerful corporations in the world are being felt everywhere and not least in the information sector itself. Thus, the Association of Data Processing Organizations (Adapso) reported that in 1978 there were approximately 3400 concerns "actively engaged in commercial corporate services" and that up to that date the industry was "highly fragmented"—not a concentrated marketplace.[35]

Adapso's executive vice-president noted, almost wistfully and with a certain unfounded romanticism, "The information products and services industry has been built by small businessmen, with innovative ideas, developing new products and services." Subsequently he added:

It is Adapso's position that the public will be best served if a large number of independent information products and services companies continue to be involved in the industry. Yet we cannot ignore the increased merger and acquisition activity, both in terms of consolidation and purchase by companies outside the information technology industry. Nor can we ignore the attempted entry of those who would have an unfair advantage in the marketplace with the ability to drive many independents out of business.[36]

INFORMATION NETWORKS: THE ULTIMATE SYNTHESIS

Summing up the discussion thus far: The manufacture of computers and the vital components of computers, the microcircuits, have become the business of a few giant companies. The use of computers to process data is being concentrated into huge service systems increasingly linked to conglomerate corporations which have large in-house computer facilities. At the same time, the data that are generated publicly by scientific, academic, and governmental bodies are being assembled into hundreds of data bases, distributed by a few corporate vendors. Other bodies of the data are being organized inside the business system itself, in the big banks and elsewhere. These data bases are being processed, packaged, and sold by firms many steps removed from communications in their alternate activities.

These movements and changes are occurring across several industries involving thousands of firms. At the same time, communication technology continues to develop and each generation of equipment far exceeds the capability of its predecessor. New models make existing facilities and processes obsolete. Not surprisingly, in such a period industrial stability and control are difficult to achieve, much less to maintain. As will be evident in later chapters, one of the expectations arising out of these multitudinous shifts is for a new equilibrium to emerge that affords the information industry and its American managers a continued opportunity for global hegemony. But for the moment, the scene bears a closer resemblance to Schumpeter's vision of the gales of "capitalist creative destruction."[37]

Yet with all this turbulence and uncertainty, a breathtaking and overarching synthesis seems to be, if not already emergent, at least present in some dim recognizable form. It takes the shape of *networks*—national and international systems linking powerful computational units, data bases, and transmission circuits. In the United states, unlike Western Europe, the network organizers are private corporations, most of which are already active and influential in one or another of several realms of modern communication.

IBM, the dominant force worldwide in computers, leads the way in creating an all-embracing communications network. A new combinatory enterprise, Satellite Business Systems (a joint venture of subsidiaries of the International Business Machines Corporation, the Comsat General Corporation, and the Aetna Life and Casualty Company has secured data transmission satellites through which it hopes to manage much of the rapidly expanding data transmission requirements of corporate business.[38] Charles P. Lecht, the President of Advanced Computer Techniques Corporation, predicts that IBM "will eventually evolve into a 'gigantic service bureau', providing computer power to users much the same way that utilities provide electricity today."[39]

The formation of a spectacular joint venture in Australia in the fall of 1980 nicely illustrates some of these possibilities. An IBM subsidiary and ten other of Australia's largest corporations have formed Business Telecommunications Services Pty. Ltd. (BTS). BTS is intended to provide business communications by satellite to the participating companies and others who may choose to use its services.

In supplying these communication services, BTS directly undercuts the Australian Federal Telecommunications Authority, Telecom. Ironically, Telecom was originally formed "to ward off telecommunications domination from abroad and coordinate a nations's assimilation of telecommunications technology."[40] The formation of BTS, according to *Computerworld*, "may indicate that IBM, through foreign subsidiaries, plans to wage war from outer space on the telecommunications monopolies or near-monopolies it finds in lucrative markets outside the U.S."[41] A different way of putting this is that IBM, utilizing satellite communication, intends to bypass national authorities which may stand in its way of engaging in profitmaking on a global scale. Anticipating this development well before its actualization, the Nora/Minc report in 1978 commented on IBM's intention to go beyond equipment manufacture and data processing: "The sovereignty stakes have shifted to control and the direction of the computer market . . . . As a controller of networks, the company [IBM] would take on a dimension extending beyond the strictly industrial sphere: it would participate, whether it wanted to or not, in the government of the plant. In effect, it has everything it needs to become one of the great regulatory systems."[42]

If this is an overblown appraisal, it is so only to the extent that IBM's path to becoming a planetary regulator is no smooth highway. As we shall find, international opposition from other industrial empires, private and public, is still to be confronted. At home, powerful corporate rivals already have indicated their willingness to challenge IBM for control of the electronic information environment. A.T.& T. has announced plans for an Advanced Communication Service (ACS) network. Xerox Corporation has proposed Xerox Telecommunications Network (Xten). And Exxon Corporation has its Qwip-based network.

The struggle between the giants is bound to provide space for some public interest. How much will depend mainly on how well organized and how broad the anti-monopoly front will be. Internationally, some foresee massive confrontations in the 1980s between United States'private international communication networks and the public networks organized in Europe and Japan to defend national (and private) interests. [43] More will be said about this in Chap. 8.

The *domestic* outcome of these emerging structures—termed by some a "network marketplace"[44]—is by no means a completed reality. Opportunity remains, as has been noted, for contestation. The likelihood that struggle will push the information technology in a social direction cannot be dismissed. All the same, some immediate consequences of what is happening are already observable.

As concentration and monopoly in communication hardware manufacturing and information-gathering, processing, and transmission have grown, so too has the gap widened in America between the information 'haves' and 'have nots'. The appearance of powerful corporate networks which integrate all levels of the informational field—from generation to dissemination—promises to deepen the existing gap into a chasm. In an article aptly titled "Information Inequality,"[45] the authors foresee a network marketplace that "will be fragmented and serve only the needs of the major multiplant businesses and industries. Most of the *Fortune 500* companies and about one-third of the medium-size industries in the nation will account for almost 80% of network usage . . .most of the smaller businesses and almost all consumers will still find the network marketplace too expensive."[45] Already "two classes of people and businesses: the information users and the information used," are distinguished. By the mid-90's, "the issue of information inequality," the same authors believe, "is likely to become one of some significant public concern, hence of political action."

Succeeding chapters will take up other manifestations of the widening gap betweeon the information 'haves' and 'have nots'. Whether another decade and a half must elapse before the issues of information inequality, and the character of information itself, can be addressed is hard to say. Much will depend on a number of struggles, public and private, national and international, inter- and intra-industry, that are bound to erupt. In fact, some have already produced sharp encounters. For the moment, the private, corporate sphere of information control waxes as the public sphere wanes. But the public has scarcely understood the developments that are underway and that are further depriving it of its informational independence. As that recognition grows, and grow it must as one of the many results of the many rivalries that cannot be contained, what now seems an inexorable push toward a totally privatized, corporative, informational environment may not in fact, be the outcome which now appears inevitable. In the chapters to follow, the various terrains on which this many-faceted contest is being waged are surveyed and analyzed.

Notes to Chapter Two

1. Angeline Pantages, "The international computer industry," *Datamation*, September 1976, p.56.
2. Rex Malik, *And tomorrow the world?* London: Millington, 1975, p. x.
3. Angeline Pantages, *op. cit.*,p. 59.
4. *Business Week*, December 17, 1979, pp.76 B & G
5. *Computerworld*, editorial, "When IBM speaks . . .", March 31, 1980. p. 28.
6. *Computerworld*, editorial, "The latest victim," October 8, 1979, p. 20.

7.   *Computerworld, April 7, 1980, p.20.*

8.   Arthur L. Robinson "Giant corporations from tiny chips grow," *Science,* May 2, 1980 *208*, pp.480–484.

9.   Arthur L. Robinson, "Perilous times for U.S. microcircuit makers," *Science,* May 9, 1980, *208* pp. 582–586.

10. James Feron, "The profits in fighter systems,"*The New York Times,* June 26, 1980, pp.D127.

11. Jake Kirchner, "CBEMA warns federal DPers of obsolescence," *Computerworld,* June 2, 1980, p.15.

12. Arthur L. Robinson, "Great corporations . . .", *op. cit.*

13. *Ibid.*

14. "Can semi-conductors survive big business?", Special Report, *Business Week,* December 3, 1979, p.66.

15. "Dividing the world market for microchips", *The New York Times,* January 29, 1980, p.D1.

16. Arthur L. Robinson, "Great corporations . . .", *op.cit.*

17. Martha E. Williams, "Database and Online Statistics for 1979", *Bulletin of the American Society for Information Science,* December 1980, 7 (2) p.27

18. Simon Nora & Alain Minc, *Computerizing society,* excerpted in *Society,* Jan./Feb. 1980 *17* (2) p.28.

19. *Information Hot-Line* October 1976, *8* (9).

20. Cees J. Hamelink, "International finances and the information industry," paper presented at the Conference on *World Communications: Decisions for the Eighties,* May 12–14, 1980, Annenberg School of Communications, Philadelphia.

21. Walter Kiechel III, "Everything you always wanted to know may soon be on-line," *Fortune,* May 5, 1980, *101* (9), p. 227.

22. Martha E. Williams, *op. cit.,* p.27

23. *Ibid* p.28.

24. Gordon Pratt, (Ed.), *Information economics.* London: Association of Special Libraries and Information Bureaus (ASLIB), and European Association of Scientific Information Dissemination Centres (EUSIDIC) 1976, p.1.

25. *Advanced Technology/Libraries,* 6 (1), January 1977.

26. Walter Kiechel III, *op. cit.*

27. *Online Review,* 1979, *3* (1) p.7.

28. *Advanced Technology/Libraries,* July 1976, *5* (7).

29. Walter Kiechel III, *op. cit.*

30. Edwin McDowell, "A data conglomerate," *The New York Times,* September 3, 1979, p. 1, SECTION III.

31. Association of Data Processing Service Organizations, Inc., et al. plaintiffs, against, Citibank, N. A., et al. defendants. United States District Court for the Southern District of New York, Adapso brief, March 26, 1980. Also, Jake Kirchner, "Adapso fighting Citibank offerings."*Computerworld*, April 7, 1980.

32. Adapso brief, *op. cit.*

33. "Exxon's next prey: IBM and Xerox,"*Business Week*, April 28, 1980, p.95.

34. Ernest Holsendolph, "Groups call for phone decontrol," *The New York Times*, August 17, 1977.

35. Jeffry Beeler, "IBM may become service bureau," *Computerworld*, March 10, 1980, p.1.

36. Jerome L. Dreyer, "Computer services: The decade ahead," *Computerworld*, January 21, 1980, pp.25–27.

37. Joseph A. Schumpeter, *Capitalism, socialism and democracy*, New York: Harper Brothers & Row, 1950.

38. Victor McElheny, "Technology," *The New York Times*, August 17, 1977.

39. Jeffry Beeler, "IBM may become service bureau," *Computerworld*, March 10, 1980, p.1.

40. "Heavy hitters sign with IBM," *Computerworld*, September 15, 1980. p.11.

41. Brad Schultz, "IBM venture spawns SBS clone down under," *Computerworld*, September 15, 1980. p. 11.

42. Nora & Minc, *op. cit.*

43. Philip A. Tenkhoff, "The networks face off,"*Computerworld*, June 16, 1980, p. 1 (SPECIAL SECTION "IN DEPTH")

44. Herbert S. Dordick, Helen G. Bradley, & Burt Nanus, "Information inequality", *Computerworld*, April 21, 1980. See also (same authors), *The emerging network marketplace*. Norwood, N.J.: Ablex, 1981.

45. *Ibid.*

chapter three

The Privatization
of Information

Paul Zurkowski of the Information Industry Association alienated the library community by accusing libraries of imposing 'an iron curtain of free information' over the land.

Library Journal
June 1, 1979, p. 1200.

While the current era is often characterized as an "information age," a more appropriate designation would take note of the fact that the privatization and commercialization of information now have become the distinguishing practices of domestic information exchange. This development is changing the way information is being viewed and handled.

Information has been sold in the past, sometimes in great volume. Yet there have always been enclaves of information generation and dissemination which either were excluded from, or ignored, in profit making. In fact, valiant battles have been waged by popular social movements to extend some of these enclaves. The motivation for these struggles, past and present, has been the belief that information is inherently social.

Now new communication technologies have made it possible to generate, process, assemble, store and disseminate enormous quantities of information. Huge private investments in the facilities to perform these tasks make it possible and profitable to handle information as a salable good. These newly offered opportunities for profit making are responsible for the quickening efforts to undermine and discredit the belief that information is a social good, a vital resource that benefits the total community when made freely available for general public use.*

Along with the attack on this belief, practices which reflect and support it also are being overturned and eliminated. In the drive toward privatization of information, the principle that "information is a commodity" plays a prominent role. Major efforts to banish the idea that information is a social good have been focused on the national government.

The national government is the country's major information generator and disseminator. Once the belief that governmental information is a public good can be disavowed, and the national governmental information supply can be corralled for private use and profit making, the *Fortune 500* have an open road toward dominion of future economic and ideological life.

THE NATIONAL GOVERNMENT AND THE PRODUCTION OF INFORMATION

In addition to a sizable and continuing growth of ordinary, day-to-day operational needs for information, for most of this century the United States Government has been confronted with systemic problems which necessitate information acquisition. Preparations for and waging of world (and local) wars, as well as efforts to stabilize the recurring economic gyrations of a privately owned and administered economy, require continuously more comprehensive and systematic information about natural resources, labor power,

*Anita R. Schiller's paper, "The Idea of the Marketplace and the Marketplace of Ideas" (On-Line Conference, San Francisco, November 13, 1980), states: "What seems most important in attempting to understand current trends, is recognizing the increasing proprietary interest in information as a profitable resource on the one hand, and the diminishing social interest in information, as a shared resource, on the other."

economic, financial, technological, geographical, and physical matters.

Mobilizing for and participating in the second world war vastly extended governmental informational involvements in research and development, largely for weapons development, resource planning and utilization, psychological warfare, and propaganda. These activities did not slacken at the end of the war. Actually, the tremendous American economic-military power in existence supplied the muscle and the wherewithal for the worldwide expansion of the United States business system.

As American economic interests pushed to the furthest reaches of the globe, the necessity for technical strength in all areas of industrial and military administration and governance demanded the continuation of massive research and development (R & D) expenditures. The government supplied them. What has become known as the "grants economy"—huge infusions of governmental funds to business and academic centers for research and development—became institutionalized.

A Brookings Institution study in 1968 paid tribute to this phenomenon:

> The initiatives the government has taken in accelerating the accumulation of new knowledge and promoting new technologies in selected areas, the responsibility for decision-making which it has assumed, the scale on which it has pursued certain objectives, and the close working relationships it has developed with private institutions—all these have been dynamic elements in the postwar development of American society.
>
> The first application of nuclear energy (to the atomic bomb) was merely the most spectacular of many technological advances achieved under government auspices during World War II. Since then there have been many others. The more dramatic include the jet airplane, supersonic flight, the nuclear-powered submarine with its inertial guidance system, high capacity computers, and sophisticated radar.

The author of this encomium justified all these "achievements" with a familiar cold war rationale: "Radar and computers are components of a variety of weapons systems and, like so many other defense items, are reminders that the nation's security continues to be a major spur to innovation. They demonstrate also the fact that, for good or ill, the cold war is in large measure a war of the laboratories."[1]

A more recent appraisal, from European sources concerned with that area's lagging information industry, saw it this way:

> The world leadership of the U.S. industry owes much to the innovative Continental market in which it flourishes, to the immense procurement power of the U.S. federal government and massive financial support which defense and space programs have given to research and development in all branches of electronics.[2]

A European study amplifies this assessment:

> The [computer] industry in the United States is the principal world supplier; it has a vast home market which it supplies almost entirely on its own. The main factor in this growth has undoubtedly been the massive orders placed by the Federal Government for more than a quarter of a century. The number of computer installations in Federal Agencies alone represents more than one-third of the total in the whole of the United States.[3]

The result of decades-long, massive governmental R & D expenditures (a congressional committee on governmental printing was informed in 1979), is "that the federal government has become the nation's chief generator of knowledge in just about every field. . .[and] as is plainly evident in Congressional hearings, the government's urgent need for information about the nation's social, economic, and technological problems is the over-arching reason why Congress in recent years appropriated between $26 and $30 billion annually for wide-ranging research projects."[4] Actually, the fiscal year budget for 1981 for the federal government requested R & D funds for 31 federal agencies, which totaled $36.1 billion.[5]

Some of the hardware and software that have come out of these huge outlays has already been noted. The focus here will be only on the *informational output* that these R & D expenditures have generated. Indicative of the magnitude of this output, a 1979 governmental study reports:

> Expenditures in the United States for the production, dissemination, and use of scientific and technical information (STI) over the last two decades increased phenomenally. . .from 1960 to 1974 STI communication expenditures increased about 323 percent, and growth is expected to continue. The Federal Government, a major

supplier and user of information, spent $4.6 billion of the $10.3 billion nationwide-total spent in 1975.[6]

These outlays, it should be emphasized, are made exclusively for the *publication and dissemination of information* derived from the far larger governmental expenditures on research and development. This publication effort, however, cannot be given enough emphasis. It provides a vast stockpile of information—some raw, some semi-processed, and much processed data—which requires varying capacities, economic and technological, for its effective application and utilization.

Given the preeminent role of corporate business in the American economy, it is to be expected that the projects most likely to utilize this informational reservoir would be undertaken by private firms expecting to make a profit. Indeed, this is the case, as for example, the formation of the private corporation COMSAT, using governmentally financed space communcations technical expertise, hardware and experience, demonstrates. (See Chap. 6, regarding remote sensing, as well.)

But the chain of relationships that this rather recent informational abundance occasions does not stop here. What has become increasingly evident is that the *information itself*, the product of public tax money, could be and is privately appropriated at its point of generation—the Government—and sold at a profit. This is an altogether new opportunity for profit making, hardly considered in the pre-World War II period. How information came into the money-making net is part of a larger story.

Corporate power, resurgent after a brief defensive period imposed on it by militant social struggles during the depression decade of the 1930s, resumed its aggressiveness during and after the war, at home and abroad. Domestically, the Government was made subordinate wherever corporate interest chose to advance its profit-making activities. The governmenntal sphere itself soon became such an area for private aggrandizement.

In 1955, a thoroughly complaisant Administration legitimized corporate forays into the governmental sector and formulated an overt policy of governmental reliance on the private sector. This quickly became the standard against which all future governmental activities were to be evaluated. The rationale for this far-reaching

penetration of corporatism into the governmental sphere was
nicely put in an executive memorandum written many years after
the fact:

> In a democratic free enterprise economic system, the Government
> should not compete with *its citizens*. The private enterprise system,
> characterized by *individual* freedom and initiative, is the primary
> source of national economic strength. In recognition of this principle,
> it has been and continues to be the general policy of the Government
> to rely on *competitive* private enterprise to supply the products and
> services it needs.[7]

Among other inaccuracies in this statement, there is the deceptive
identification of individuals and citizens as the beneficiaries of a policy which is formulated for corporate objectives and interests.

Implementations of and additions to this policy have occurred
regularly since the time it was first announced in a 1955 Bureau of
the Budget Bulletin. The most recent revision is found in Circular
No. A-76 Revised, issued by the Office of Management and Budget
on March 29, 1979. The central policy aim set forth in this document
is: "*Rely on the Private Sector*. The Government's business is not to
be in business. Where private sources are available, they should be
looked to first to provide the commercial or industrial goods and
services needed by the Government to act on the public's behalf."[8]

Initially, this policy was not designed specifically for the governmental information sector. It was intended to affect the general
procurement of goods and services increasingly used by a greatly
expanded State apparatus. Still, it was inevitable that the policy
would be applied to information as that field of governmental activity, fueled by the enormous R & D outlays, became increasingly significant. What has occurred, in fact, is that governmentally funded
information generation has become a rich and sought-after treasure
trove. Developments in recent years in this field are understood
best, therefore by examining how this prize is being appropriated
and who is doing the appropriating.

The appropriation process extends from the initial securing of
federal funds to generate information, to the actual printing of the
newly generated information (and more recently, to taping and
filming), and to its dissemination and utilization. At each stage commercial elements, fortified with the doctrine of "reliance on the private sector," are seeking to insert and advance their interests.

Data base producers, information packagers and service suppliers, and many large companies with specific informational interests—e.g., mining, agribusiness, oil, etc.—are moving quickly and aggressively, within and outside political and legislative channels, to preempt the national information supply produced with federal money, and the machinery for its dissemination, as well.

An Ad Hoc Committee, advising the Joint Committee on Printing of the U.S. Congress, in its 1979 report set forth the overarching policy question that is being decided almost by default: "Should the information generated by the government," asked the Committee, "be considered as an economic good to be dealt with in purely economic terms, or as a social good to be dealt with in purely social terms, or a combination of both?"[9]

The private sector has no doubt whatsoever how this question should be answered. Paul Zurkowski, president of the Information Industry Association, in a paper prepared for the National Commission on Libraries and Information Science in 1974, wrote:

> The marriage of the profit motive to the distribution of information is the single most important development in the information field since Carnegie began endowing libraries with funds to make information in books and journals more widely available to the public . . . [Consequently] the government of the U.S. has the responsibility to assure that the opportunity for private sector initiatives is expanded and not contracted.[10]

Another voice of the Information Industry, James B. Adler, president of the private Congressional Information Service, before a congressional committee considering a revision of the law regulating government printing, said flatly:

> One of the points that we are trying to make, Mr. Chairman, is that just as it is presently JCP [Joint Committee on Printing] policy to encourage the use of private facilities in the printing of Government documents, it should be the policy of the Committee to encourage the use of private facilities in the distribution of public information wherever that is practical and consistent with the public interest.[11]

Adler emphasized further that a revised law should be explicit on this matter: "We believe that as a matter of policy Congress should write in policy guidance up front that says that private capabilities which can be used for the public good should be considered in constructing Government printing and distribution activities."[12] The chairman of the Congressional subcommittee, Congressman Hawkins, inquired at this point: "So you are really asking us to go beyond the current law?" Adler replied: "Yes Sir."[13]

The efforts of the relatively recently organized private information industry (IIA) firms to seize the existing public informational stockpile and undertake its further production, processing, and distribution—the IIA is generally content to allow the Government to continue to spend substantial tax moneys to finance the generation of information—are being felt in many undertakings that until a very short time ago were considered non-profit-making activities.

Commercial interest is on the offensive. So much is this so, that the generally unexcitable and rarely aggressive American Library Association, through its Executive Director, made a critical assessment of the direction in which decision-making over public information seems to be moving. Events of the last ten years, Robert Wedgworth stated, "have awakened many Americans to recognition that their government is theirs and the information it provides is available for the asking."

Though these are both questionable assertions, Wedgworth went on to say that a threat to this information's accessibility is

Posed by a group of companies whose services are based on new developments in computer technology, micro-graphics, and telecommunications. While we have to live in the same environment and make use of the service of these companies, I am quite interested in their contention that the federal government as the largest producer and disseminator of information in the U.S. should channel most of its publishing and distribution functions through the private sector rather than through agencies such as the GPO, the federal depository library system, and the National Technical Information Service. . . .Yet in some instances this argument fails to recognize that they may be seeking access to information already collected and organized at public expense. It is maintained that these companies can plan and distribute better quality products more effectively than the government. Yet many of the agencies that are the targets of these arguments, such as the National Institute of Health, *have a statutory mission to print and disseminate information produced with public funds for the public benefit, distributing the cost to all taxpayers rather than to those who are in most urgent need of the information.* This may be the single most controversial issue in the na-

tional program for library and information services that we have
seen proposed over the last several years.[14]

Wedgworth's statement may be overly generous in its assessment
of the Government's responsibility and accessibility to the people.
Hegemonic control of governmental information by the private sector has never been absent in the United States. What is different
now, however, is the shift from indirect to direct control, accom-
plished through the market mechanism: the private sale and purchase of government information

Wedgworth is on the mark, though, when he emphasizes the implications for and the peril to *general* accessibility of information
when commercial initiatives take over and organize distribution on
an individual ability-to-pay basis. When this occurs, not only do
those with the ability to pay gain advantaged access, but eventually—and, ultimately most importantly—they become the arbi-
ters of what kind of information shall be produced and what is made
available. The market unsentimentally yet inexorably confers this
authority on those with the fatter bank accounts. Wedgworth is
correct, also, in believing that a vital issue is involved. It is no less
than: Who will direct what kinds of information the Government
will produce in the years and decades ahead? To what purposes that
information will be put will be another basic decision made in the
same manner.

Actually, the survival of many frail but crucial institutions which
have served to protect or advance the public interest is, if not immediately at stake, threatened. Increasing reliance on the private
sector and market forces to organize, process, and disseminate information, already is beginning to erode the functions of several
public institutions.

These public activities, it need be repeated, have rarely offered
adequate service, and often have provided institutional reinforce-
ment for the status quo. Yet they have also nourished a conception
of public interest and social service and, at certain historical junc-
tures, have given support and in turn been supported by progressive social currents. Transforming these institutions into market
structures—the objective of the IIA and its promoters—is to re-
move from society those few agencies capable of systemic meliora-
tion and humanization.

Access to and commercial disposal of the already large and continuously growing governmental information hoard are the objectives of the for-profit forces in the economy. In working toward this goal, the governmental informational structures and the many intermediary networks that transmit some of this information are the targets for private takeover or serious reductions in capability.

In what follows, some of these developments are briefly reviewed. Justification for any incompleteness in the discussion is that the onslaughts are relatively recent. They are ongoing and quite complex in their detail; uncertainties are numerous; outcomes are not predestined, and in many cases not yet very clear. Still, some patterns, not very promising to the public's need to know, are beginning to take shape.

The private attack is characterized by an insistence that information is a commodity and that those who wish to use it should pay for it. The battle swirls around those structures and institutions, in the Government and outside it, directly engaged in information generation, publishing (in the most comprehensive sense), and dissemination.

INFORMATION GENERATION

The process of information generation is under commercial siege and private interests have encroached substantially on what once were nonprofit activities producing a wide range of information. Federal laboratories, for example, which once undertook directly a good portion of the Government's research work, have been neglected—relatively and absolutely. An ever larger share of the Federal R & D outlays are channeled to corporate laboratories and academic centers which are developing close commercial connections.[15]

Another side of the post-World War II decline in direct, Federal engagement in research and development work is revealed in a study prepared more than a decade ago. It noted that "the business share of federal research and development work. . .has increased from 26.9 percent of federal expenditures in 1954 to 65.1 percent in 1964 . . . [and conversely] since 1940, the use of federal research and development funds by people employed directly by the government has grown less rapidly than has the government's aggregate program."[16] These trends have continued into the 1970s and nothing on the horizon in the '80s promises to reverse them.

A study published in *Science* reported that "of the 610,000 scientists and engineers engaged in R & D in 1979, more than three-fifths were employed by industry. In dollar terms, industry performs about 72 percent of the total.[17] One of the consequences of this privatization of research (the bulk of which is financed by public money) is that a capability of noncommerical, independent evaluation of R & D outputs is weakened, if not eliminated, as the Federal R & D capacity atrophies. An informational consequence of equal significance is that the information derived from these expenditures on research and development may fail to find its way back into the stream of public information. It may be appropriated by the private sector and further promote the aggrandizement of its appropriators.

One facet of the general tendency of private appropriation of public information is the widespread use of private consultants to perform research and evaluative studies for the government. This is a development strongly encouraged by the OMB policy first enunciated in 1955, which stipulated that there should be government reliance on the private sector for the goods and services required for public administration and performance.

This phenomenon reveals a curious aspect of the alleged age of information. All the attention to the informational character of the society notwithstanding, even the number of private consultants on the public payroll remains unknown. The chairman of the Senate subcommittee on Civil Service and General Services observed in 1979 that "we still do not know how many consultants the Government uses, how much they are paid, or what benefit the Government derives from these particular services."[18]

The amounts involved in these practices, however, are far from trivial. A study conducted by the *Washington Post*, and reported in *Documents to the People*, "showed that the Government spent more than $9.3 billion for consultants and [consulting] contracts, and that 68% of the 16,101 research and consulting contracts advertised in 1979 were awarded without competition."[19]

After this information was published, the *Post* reported that at a Cabinet level meeting at the White House, the Director of the Office of Management and Budget (OMB) "directed all agencies to improve control over the hiring of consultants" but its efforts to enforce this policy are hampered because "OMB has not been able to find out how many outside consultants the government is using and what they are being paid!"[20]

What is known, however, is that the pervasive use of private consultants multiplies the obstacles in the way of public information availability and contributes to further informational inequality in the nation at large. The Ad Hoc Advisory Committee to the Joint Congressional Committee on Printing touched, albeit lightly, on this:

> Many government agencies, in contracting for research/ development and consultant studies, specifically permit the private contractor to copyright the results of this federally funded research . . . The result of this contract procedure is that the research findings are not routinely listed in the MONTHLY CATALOG [the Governmental listing of U.S. publications] and are not distributed to depository libraries. In fact, government-funded libraries and information clearing houses often have to purchase such contract reports from private commercial sector publishers.[21]

With this neat arrangement, private informational enterprises are twice blessed, and public knowledgeability is drastically limited.

Another consequence—perhaps more egregious still—of the use of private consultants to handle and assess public functions can only be mentioned here. This involves the quality and character of the findings and recommendations of private firms and individuals on matters concerning the largest issues of social policy.

It is carrying temptation well beyond ordinary limits to institutionalize arrangements whereby profit-making organizations are called upon to assess and advise on public policy making. When, for example, the Treasury Department of the United States Government asks the leading private accounting firm, Price Waterhouse & Co., and "at least three major New York investment banking firms to help the Government scrutinize the financial rescue plan submitted by the Chrysler Corporation,"[22] the mind boggles at the flagrant disregard for the potential of outrageous conflict-of-interest.

WEAKENING THE GOVERNMENT PUBLISHING AND DISSEMINATION FUNCTION

To recapitulate, a massive shift of Federal R & D expenditures from governmental laboratories to corporate facilities and private contractors has occurred since World War II. Simultaneously, there has been an increased use by the Government of private consultants that offer advice and make studies for governmental policy direction. Both of these developments have led to huge amounts of government-financed data and information which escape or are diverted from freely accessible public channels of distribution. Sometimes the findings embodied in this documentation, processed, and 'enriched', are priced prohibitively and become available only to already-knowledgeable and affluent groups and individuals—mostly the business community—directly concerned with or affected by the information. Less influential and prosperous groups may be excluded and may not even know the information is available.

More recently, the arrangements governing the organization, publication, and dissemination of the information that remains under governmental control—a still very considerable body of data—have begun to undergo significant changes. Though these changes are still occurring and are not easily explicable without detailed elaboration, some general tendencies are observable. What seems to be happening, perhaps accelerating, is the continued weakening of the public publishing function, along with a growing effort to commercialize the Government's information product.

In what follows, it will be useful to keep in mind two separate kinds of developments. One involves the outcomes of the growing influence, deliberately applied, of market forces on governmental publishing and information dissemination. This has been mentioned already but will be elaborated in the subseqent discussion. The other changes involve governmental reorganizations in the fields of public printing and document dissemination. These are being proposed and implemented under the general framework of the revision and amendment of Title 44, United States Code, which establishes the rules for the administration of public printing services and the distribution of public documents.

This latter area of change is affecting the actual organization of governmental entities. To be sure, the two developments are related. In these pages, however, most attention will be given to the impact of market forces on the public publishing and dissemination functions. Where these impacts are detectable, also, in proposed legislative reorganization of governmental entities, they will be noted briefly.

Impacts from these separate but related developments are especially evident in the extensive efforts to diminish the domain of the Government Printing Office (GPO); in the promotion and growth of the National Technical Information Service as a rival to the GPO, and in the continued deficiencies and frailty of the national depository library system. A brief consideration of each of these mini-information wars, follows.

THE GROWING TRIALS OF THE GOVERNMENT PRINTING OFFICE

The Government Printing Office came into being in 1861.[23]. For most of its existence, it handled the bulk of the national government's printing, binding, and distribution of documents requirements in in-house, governmentally owned facilities. All this changed with the tremendous increase of government printing, precipitated by the outbreak of the Second World War. From 1940 on, under the stimulus of heavy defense requirements for printing, commercial firms were increasingly utilized under contract. This practice continued after the war and by 1979, two-thirds of the printing contracts from the GPO went to the private sector and their value exceeded $425 million annually.[24]

The growing appetite of the private information industry firms, however, is not directed especially to the printing function of the GPO, although some commercial companies certainly are not indifferent to that source of revenue. The IIA is concerned mainly with generating, processing, and distributing the government's information. It seeks also to undertake such functions as assembling, indexing, document delivery, and disseminating information in new formats, such as microfiche. It also has been intent on restricting the Government Printing Office from entering into the new fields of information handling and packaging.

To the extent that the IIA is successful in limiting the GPO's activities in processing the output of government agencies while expanding the commercial sector's role, the private information firms also gain distributional control of a tremendous storehouse of publicly financed information.

The economic potential here is substantial. Yet still greater long-range benefits accrue to the for-profit, information sector. *Changing the direction and emphasis of the Government's information activity from public to private, and from social to commercial, is a key to transforming the role of information in the entire economy.* The Government is the central information generator in the system and "the largest user of computer technology in the world."* Once it begins to operate with commercial criteria for information production and dissemination, social considerations in the production and use of information begin to disappear throughout the society.

Accordingly, the issue of charging the user for information has become the focal point of the commercial offensive against the public information sector, and against the GPO and libraries, in particular. The commercial information companies insist, first, that all publicly financed information should be sold and retailed at a price no less than its cost of production. Their second demand is that the for-profit sector should become the main distributional channel.

> The information industry [the IIA asserts,] is a major growth industry of the future providing exciting new products and services today which only yesterday were unavailable. *The capabilities of this industry should be relied on today even in cases where government information activities were undertaken when the industry was not recognized to be capable of providing these services.*[25]

In short, many informational activities and functions which hitherto have been public now, according to the IIA, should become commercial and profit producing. In implementing this objective, the Government Printing Office is first in line for sharply reduced responsibilities. The process of contraction has begun, though not abruptly nor entirely visibly.

Among the elements that assist the IIA and its supporters in their efforts to transform public information dissemination into commercial enterprise are the longstanding deficiencies of the GPO, which are now much more in evidence because information has come to play so large a role in the economy. For one thing, "it is not the central source of government documents for the public that it is supposed to be." For another, "there is much that GPO should be doing that it is not doing at all."[26] Both of these assessments are the direct consequences of the limited, narrow view of public information that has characterized the administration of the GPO for a long time.

---

*President Carter, Letter of Transmittal to Congress on the Report of the White House Conference on Library and Information Services, The White House, September 26, 1980.

Administrators within the GPO have had little enthusiasm for carrying out a policy of supplying the public with socially useful information. "It is clear that to its officials," Shawn Kelly writes, "the Government Printing Office is not considered primarily a source of valuable information, but rather a self-sustaining mail-order business."[27] Still, the GPO's troubles and limitations are not by any means all self-induced. Congress has seen to it that the organization has been underfinanced for years, as well as having made it official policy to contract out the bulk of government printing to private printers. Thus, the rigidities and inadequacies of the GPO, imposed and internalized, make it an easy target for the adversaries of a genuinely public information service.

THE NATIONAL TECHNICAL INFORMATION SERVICE (NTIS)

One of the ways in which the control of public information publishing and distribution has gradually been separated from the GPO has been through the establishment, in 1970, of what has become a rival governmental unit, the National Technical Information Service (NTIS). This agency was given a mandate to publish and make available the government's scientific and technical information output. The NTIS resides, not by chance, in the Department of Commerce, the agency which explicitly is assigned the promotion of the business community's interests.

To describe the growth, activities, and influence of the NTIS would require a volume of its own. Here it is sufficient, I believe, to note that the NTIS has been utilized, not necessarily intentionally, as a force promoting the further commercialization of government information. It has done this, first, by introducing and following steadfastly the principle of selling at commercial prices all the documentation it makes available. Its second contribution to commercialization of government information has been indirect but also damaging. It has served to weaken the position of the GPO as the primary government agency engaged in information handling and dissemination.

The insertion of NTIS into the governmental information network has created the divided and weakened information authority that now exists. A 1979 Congressional Research Service report, based on a survey of governmental information activities, noted:

NTIS is somewhat of an enigma. While the major criteria for submission of documents to NTIS are that they be technical and/or scientific in nature, the survey responses demonstrated that there may be some documents which could just as well be under GPO control, *with easier access by the general public.*

At the same time, the report continued, other agencies "are failing to notify GPO of the documents produced through sources other than GPO," and consequently, "there appears to exist no comprehensive source of the most basic information on Federal publications."[28]

Summing up the ambiguities created by the informational activities of NTIS, the report posed these questions:

How does the public gain access to an index of all publications in the NTIS system? Do the Depository libraries receive copies as part of a free distribution system? What procedures do the agencies follow to determine whether a document should go to GPO or NTIS, or both? Are restrictions placed by NTIS on the agencies with regards to the distribution other than through NTIS?

Does NTIS claim copyright on classes of documents within the system [and finally] to what extent is NTIS in competition with GPO, [and] if there is competition, does it diminish GPO's effectiveness?[29]

Not a result of NTIS' activity, but relevant to the issue of leakage in the national public information system, a 1980 congressional study produced astonishment at the disarray and sieve-like quality of the record of the government's informational output. It reported:

Without an accurate inventory of just what is published by an agency, thousands of useful publications never are forwarded to GPO as is now required by law for inclusion in the official listing of government publications in the GPO's Monthly Catalog. This catalog listing is absolutely essential for librarians and the public to know what is available. . .*perhaps as high as 40 percent of the publications generated* by Federal agencies with tax dollars never are included in the Monthly Catalog so that the public may know they exist and have access to them.[30]

Bertram Gross, in his unique study, *Friendly Fascism*, commented on this gap in the governmental information inventory and views it as part of a much wider information hole that affects almost everyone in the country.[31]

The efforts of NTIS, supported by the Office of Management and Budget, to broaden its influence at the expense of the GPO and to extend a 'sales philosophy' to all government information, continue unabated. For example, in a draft bulletin, No. 78, dated June 30, 1978, the OMB *ignored the GPO completely* and proposed to make the NTIS the agency responsible for disseminating scientific and technical information which resulted from federally funded research and development activities.[32] Following objections of university and documents librarians across the country, as well as critical comments from some other agencies in the Government itself,[33] a revised draft circular on *Improved Management and Dissemination of Federal Information* was released for comment in June 1980.

The preeminent role of NTIS in the dissemination of scientific and technical information was reasserted. The draft also included a curious definition of "public information." Its "distinguishing characteristic," according to the OMB circular, "is that the [governmental] agency actively seeks, in some fashion, to disseminate such information or otherwise make it available to the public."[34] In sum, public information is what any governmental agency deems it appropriate to inform the public about.

The policy principles enunciated in the 1980 OMB draft circular are especially illuminating. Commercialization of government-produced information is the central policy objective. Several of the principles set forth make this quite explicit. For example, Principle (a) announces that "public information held by the Federal Government shall be made available to the public in an effective, efficient and *economic* manner." Principle (c) states: "Information is not a free good." It softens this dictum somewhat, by adding, "however, no member of the public should be denied access to public information held by the Federal Government solely because of economic status. In particular, the Federal Government shall rely upon the depository library system to provide free citizen access to public information."

This assurance is less of a guarantee than it purports to be. The next section, on depository libraries, makes the point that the depository system itself is being subjected to commercial pressure. If the Information Industry Association and the Office of Management and Budget have their way—and little seems to stand in their path at this time—depository libraries will be no less market oriented than NTIS.

Principle (d) states that "information available through a mechanism other than the depository library system shall, unless required by other law or program objectives, be made available at a price which recovers all costs to the government associated with the dissemination of such information." And finally, Principle (e) insists that "The Federal Government shall, in accordance with OMB circular A-76, and where not inconsistent with law, *place maximum feasible reliance upon the private sector to disseminate* public information."[35]

The 1980 OMB draft circular on the management and dissemination of federal information may well be revised again. But what is unlikely to be changed, and what actually may be strengthened, are the endorsement and encouragement, implemented in policy, of the privatization and commercialization of government information.

THE GOVERNMENT LIBRARY DEPOSITORY SYSTEM

The growth of the NTIS *inside* the federal structure as a commercial vendor of government information weakens not only the GPO as the primary agency responsible for information coordination. Another institution as well, in the public information network, is affected. This is the government depository system. Though limited arrangements for the deposit of U.S. Government journals and documents were in effect in the early 19th century, "the real basis of the institution of depositories" was created in a series of resolutions and acts of Congress in the immediate pre-Civil War years, 1857–1859. Amended and expanded by congressional action since, the depository system now in operation "provides for a class of libraries in the United States in which certain Government publications are deposited for the use of the public."[36] There are now 1230 institutions designated as government depository libraries, several located in each state.

There is considerable autonomy in each depository library to select the government documents and publications it feels are of most interest and value to the specific constituency it serves. However, the general intent of the system is to have available, in accessible sites, in every state of the union, several depositories which are able to provide the general public with *comprehensive access to the full spectrum* of governmentally produced information. The depository system, regardless of how actively it has been utilized, must be regarded as an important democratic facility at the disposal of the community.

Any development, therefore, that weakens the system—impairs its capabilities by reducing its comprehensiveness—is not a trivial matter. The informational well-being of the general public is affected. When the availability of government documents becomes uncertain because an unknown amount of material is siphoned off by an agency inside the government, operating commercially, such as NTIS, as well as other massive leakages,* the depository system is undermined.

It is undermined because it no longer is assured of receiving a complete inventory of government documentation. Moreover, it sometimes is unable to afford the prices charged by NTIS if it wishes to secure that agency's publications in the marketplace.[37]

Besides the NTIS, there is another, possibly more serious and growing threat to the depository system. These are the efforts of the private information firms to shift the distribution of documentation to the depositories to a market arrangement. Indicative is the proposal the IIA put before the Joint Congressional Committee on Printing in 1979: "Our Association fully supports continued and increased assistance for depositories; however, we believe that support should be in a more direct form, rather than indirect subsidies."

What the Association had in mind here is the replacement of the flow of free government publications to the depositories--labelled "subsidy" by the IIA--with cash payment which would permit the depositories to choose privately-prepared information packages.

Speaking for IIA, James Adler argued:

> At the moment, the depository requires a library to accept its subsidy [sic] from the government in the form of documents. If it wishes

---

*According to a study by Coopers & Lybrand, a private consulting firm, "GPO performs only about 50% of all government printing . . . . GPO distributes about 40% of the documents it prints." *Analysis and Evaluation of Selected Government Printing Office Operations*, prepared by Coopers & Lybrand, an Independent Consulting Firm, Washington, D.C., under the auspices of the Joint Committee on Printing, Washington, D.C., 1979, p. xix.

to make use of any private competing services, it must use its own funds exclusively to buy these additional services. We are suggesting that it would not strain the ingenuity of the staff and members of Congress, to create any one of a number of alternative systems which would provide a wider choice to depositories in terms of choosing the form and source of the documents they receive than the present system provides.[38]

Replying to this view, Donald Koepp, University Librarian at Princeton, declared on behalf of the Association of Research Libraries:

I would most emphatically not want a subsidy in lieu of the depository for all sorts of reasons. I have a distinct feeling that that would eventually erode into a situation where our control over the material would evaporate; I emphasize one of the most important things for us is control which permits us to identify the existence of a document.[39]

The IIA's proposal would, if enacted, no longer assure a national uniform core of material, available to the public in the many libraries situated all around the country. The Association of Research Libraries' representative noted further that "probably 50 percent of the basic publications of the Government Printing Office are selected by almost any library, any depository of any size in the country. The variations is [sic] at the margin." Clearly, the emphasis on "choice" for depositories that the IIA stresses is a secondary matter at best. The vital need is to protect the 50 percent uniform core.

There is another, not-so-apparent, but likely consequence if the direct cash payment proposal of the IIA were to be accepted. It would introduce the market mechanism into the depository system itself. The demand for government publications at each depository, under a cash subsidy arrangement, would become a site for competing interests to express their preferences. Little imagination is required to see which interests would predominate in an environment where *Fortune 500* criteria and influence prevail. This expressed preference would, in turn, feed back into the total information generation process and push it still further in the direction of the corporate economy's informational interest.

In the matter of cash payments in lieu of documents to the depository libraries, to date the IIA's views have not prevailed. The provision that was introduced originally in the National Publications

Act of 1979 was rejected.[40] The Act itself, retitled the National Publications Act of 1980, died in the 96th Congress. Still, it would be a mistake to believe that the drive against the social use of public information has slackened. Market criteria are being promoted heavily throughout the system of government document distribution. Though the specific mechanisms are still in formative stages, and the full impact of the shift is yet to be felt, there is reason enough to have anxiety over the enfeeblement of the general system.

The national depository library system, along with other institutional structures representing the public's access to and use of tax-supported governmental information, are pressured relentlessly. Inside the Government the NTIS, and outside the private information sector, tirelessly promote and extend private and commercial arrangements for information distribution.

Withal, the Carter Administration, reporting to Congress on the recommendations of the 1979 White House Conference on Library and Information Services, "promised to strengthen the role of the federal depository system in providing access to government information and pointed to gains made already in this area."[41]

COUNTERVAILING CURRENTS

The trends and changes noted above, which affect the availability of documentation resulting from Federal R & D and other expenditures, reveal a profound shift that threatens an already none-too-secure structure of public information accessibility. Institutions long established to assure public information service have been weakened, disoriented, and sometimes reorganized. Privatization of formerly public functions proceeds almost uninterruptedly under the stimulus of an energetic industry sector as well as a general climate favorable to unchecked private enterprise last observable in the 1920s.

The consequences are twofold. Accessibility to the general public of federally produced information becomes increasingly problematic. At the same time, closure to the public of all kinds of governmental information is occurring more and more systematically. In the latter case, for example, *The New York Times* reported that in the Spring 1980 session of Congress, more than 20 legislative proposals were introduced "that would limit access to Government information."[42]

Matching Congress' moves against its own constituents' vital information needs, federal agencies are making their own substantial contributions to the public's informational deprivation. For example, the Federal Communications Commission, assigned the mandate to protect the public interest in the field of broadcasting, proposed to eliminate the requirement that radio stations "keep detailed logs on their broadcasts for public inspection."[43] In the absence of such records, the ability of public interest groups, and individuals as well, to monitor easily the performance of broadcasters is severely impaired. Social accountability of broadcasting, or any other public function, requires a record available to public scrutiny.

Let me include a personal account of the difficulty now experienced in obtaining what should be easily available information. Almost immediately upon reading that the FCC had published a study, "Preliminary Report on Prospects for Additional Networks," in early 1980, I wrote to the Chairman of the Subcommittee on Communications, of the House of Representatives' Committee on Interstate and Foreign Commerce. This subcommittee oversees the Federal Communications Commission. A short time thereafter, I was informed by the Committee's counsel that the FCC "is out of copies of the network study related report." I then inquired of our University's government publications division, which happens also to be a government publications depository, if the document was available. The following reply was received promptly from a University government publications Librarian:

> The FCC report presents real problems. I called the FCC, and they recognized the title immediately, but they also confirmed that they do not have any copies left. They also confirmed that the report was *not* sent as a depository item to libraries.
>
> They did say that copies of their reports could be purchased from the Downtown Copy Center, 1114 21st St. N.W. Washington, D.C., phone 202-452-1422. (This is a private outfit.) I called the copy center and they too recognized the title; they will provide it at 9 cents per page; the whole report, however, is 1611 pages long; thus the total charge (including $12.82 postage) would be over $150.
>
> I also contacted Government Documents department at San Diego State [University], mainly because they belong to the 'Docu-

ments' Expediting program which is one way non-depository items can be acquired. They do not have it either. They are going to make inquiries through the Documents Expediting project, but they didn't seem very hopeful.[44]

This personal chronicle seems to represent the condition of public information accessibility at this time though eventually, in this instance, the report did come into the depository library on microfiche. If these are the experiences of someone academically close to the field of information, who is assisted by a skilled librarian, in one of the country's distinguished research libraries, what may be said of the information options of less favorably situated citizens?

The evidence of increasing privatization of and barriers to governmentally generated information is not necessarily confirmatory of Bertram Gross' vision of an imminent *Friendly Fascism.* Yet it would be equally mistaken to view these developments as inconsequential or reflective of the normal ebb and flow of public affairs.

However, counterbalancing forces are at work. Currently, they lack strength; still, there are reasons to believe that the principle of freely available public information may muster more support in the time ahead. For one thing, the national government itself is no monolith on this matter. There are disagreements among the many agencies in the federal structure over the desirability of present trends. While the departments most associated with the private sector and most heavily involved with the information industry's products are generally accepting, if not promoting, of the commercialization of government information, other agencies either try to adhere to the earlier formula of public accessibility, or, less concerned with principle, wish all the same to keep the information function under their own wing.

Those federal departments striving hardest to withhold information from the public, and accepting eagerly the commercialization of what they agree to release, are the most powerful and heavily financed agencies of the Government. They are also, not incidentally, those parts of the bureaucracy most closely associated with or actually integral to the power centers of the system overall. Not unexpectedly, the Department of Commerce, which houses the NTIS, the Department of Defense, NASA, and OMB are most outspoken in their opposition to widening public information accessibility.[45]

Whatever the internal lack of agreement in its various subdivisions, the Government, acting under executive direction, may be expected to reconsider its present acceptance of the splintered authority over federal information and the consequent huge leakages of documentation from the system's retrieval capacity. The necessity for rapid, comprehensive information, in accessible data bases, under unified means of accessing, will intensify as crises erupt in the future. In this very real sense, information fragmentation imperils systemic survival.

Yet there are very strong potential negative consequences of unification, centralization, and deliverability of information. Better organization of information can serve repressive as well as liberatory ends. Given the present structure and use of power in the United States, there is slight prospect that the emanicipatory side of information mobilization will be favored at this time. Still, this cannot be taken for granted. The insistence on maintaining intact, freely accessible public information resources cannot be lessened.

Still another factor that eventually may trigger policy reversals in the information field is the rapidly changing structure of the information industry itself and the conflicts this is producing. In Chapter 2 some of these developments were reviewed. Summarizing these briefly, the competitive nature of the industry, apparent in its early years, is disappearing. The period in which relatively small and extremely vigorous companies were innovating and producing new formats, new hardware, and new packages of information which, in many instances, had not been available earlier in usable forms, is coming to a close. Following a familiar, capitalist developmental course, the movement to merger, consolidation, and conglomeration accelerates.

Both familiar and newly arrived information behemoths are on the prowl. The information industry itself is anxiety ridden. Smaller firms are confronting giant structures. Consequently, their need and willingness to participate in anti-monopoly coalitions are not matters of choice but of survival. A coalition of this kind *may* be an outcome of the developments considered here.

The subversion of what Gross calls the "democratic machinery" has proceeded rapidly in recent years. Yet much of this machinery, however disabled, remains in place. More important, it still possesses substantial allegiance and significant numbers of practitioners. Suggestive of the latent democratic forces in American society,

especially in the public information field, which may yet be mobilized and activated, are the libraries and their staffs and friends.
Assuredly, the library sector is no Exxon of power in the economy.
Yet it cannot be disregarded entirely as a social force with deep
roots in the community.

Librarianship has been grounded historically in the idea of public
service. The commercialization of information runs counter to this
deeply embedded principle. Accordingly libraries, and librarians
too, are being subjected to the pressures and compulsions of the
drive to extend the market into their domain. What is happening to
public libraries, as computerization is introduced and market forces
are encouraged as the means to finance the newer systems, is a
story of its own. It parallels many of the developments that have
been described here affecting government information.

An indication of the concern these trends are producing is revealed, in part, in some of the resolutions adopted at the first White
House Conference on Library and Information Service (WHCLIS),
convened in November 1979. At least four of the conference's resolutions were related directly to the professions's insistence that
free public access to information be maintained and extended. For
example, in resolutions supporting a national information policy,
"the right of access, without charge or fee to the individual, to all
public and publicly supported libraries" was advocated. Similarly,
Congress was asked "to continue to foster broad public participation in the federal government by subsidizing the sale of documents
and maintaining the system of regional depository libraries." And
another resolution "asks for the study and implementation of a national information policy that guarantees all citizens equal and full
access to publicly funded library and information services, that en-
sures federal agencies will do everything they can to make these
services available.[46]

Each of these resolutions collides with the positions advocated by
the IIA, now being implemented by governmental action. Though
the opposition at this time remains limited, apparently confined to
the library profession (there, too, it is by no means a dominant current), it is at least imaginable that other public sector fields, also
threatened by these developments, may join in common cause
against the information privatizers and marketeers.

One more development affecting the pace of privatization and
concentration of control of public information may be mentioned.

These are the continuing and far-reaching changes occurring in information and communication technology. Again, this is a double-edged situation. In some instances, the new technology encourages mergers and combinations which enable higher capacities of information handling to be utilized more efficiently and to extend the control of already-giant structures. At the same time, the possibility for long-term consolidation and stabilization are reduced, at least temporarily. The uncertainties attendant on a rapidly changing technology arise from the possibile obsolescence of facilities, from the loss or gain of markets, and possibly from the entrance of new competitors. How the balance eventually will be struck in the information field is not completely predictable at this time. The strength and commanding positions of the giants in the communications sector—especially the equipment producers and media owners—suggest an eventual absorption of the new technologies into the hands of a few super-corporations.

Already a few media combines, including Warner Amex, Westinghouse, The Times Mirror Company, and Time, Inc., have a commanding position in the new cable TV industry.[47] Yet surprises are not out of the question. The uncertainty and instability created, to say nothing of the appearance of continuously enlarged monopolies, create opportunities for debate and public resistance.

The efforts to rewrite the Communications Act of 1934 are richly suggestive of these potential conflicts and ambiguities. Most of the debate and opposition over the rewrite have arisen from competing economic groups—broadcasters, hardware producers, data processors—whose interests collide. But in the attempts to smooth out differences, or at least to minimize disagreement of these major, private interests, the opportunity for public interests to be expressed, if not respected, is sometimes possible. Pertinent here, is the concern of the smaller firms in the information processing and computer services industries about being driven out of business by the few communication behemoths, A.T.&T. in particular.

This fear reflects itself in pressure on Congress to protect their existence. This was manifest early in 1980, when "four trade associations representing a substantial percentage of the U.S. computer industry . . . jointly demanded that the House [of Representatives] Communications Subcommittee make further changes to curb A.T.&T.'s monopoly power in its pending rewrite of the Communications Act of 1934 . . . . If the proposed changes aren't adopted, 'we intend to block passage of the bill and will try to un-seat the legislators responsible', CCIA [Computer and Communications Industry Association] President Jack Biddle said."[48]

If this threat were indeed carried out, the ensuing battle would inevitably draw in public interest forces who would seek to broaden the conflict into larger frameworks of public access and general availability of information.

Should a popular, anti-information monopoly opposition actually develop in the future, it may still be more than countered by the information complex. This grouping seems intent on forging still stronger ties within its own already-powerful coalition of corporate, military, and academic interests. A former presidential science adviser, now a vice-president for science and technology of Exxon, calls for "a new synthesis of national, corporate and academic resources to sustain innovation"[49]—the expected outcome of expenditures on research.

Largely to expedite this 'general synthesis', the proposed 1981 Federal budget for research and development allocated an increase of 21 percent to the Department of Defense's "basic research" funds, which, it is hoped, will enable the military to mount "a dedicated effort to re-cement the relations" with the academic community.[50]

The integration of the academic research community into the information complex will be promoted further by contracting enrollments and increasingly limited funds for general education. These developments are likely to lead to further channeling of the production of information as well as to its tighter control and limited accessibility. Major universities are beginning to consider seriously engaging in commercial development of the findings coming out of their academic laboratories.[51]

What is occurring therefore, in the information field, is a pincers movement against the public's knowledgeability. On one side, outputs of public information are being transferred to the marketplace and priced accordingly. On the other, information and message-making from private, corporate sources are expanding and reaching new, large, and national audiences. It is to this second phenomenon—the emergence of dense networks of private message making—that the next chapter is devoted.

Notes to Chapter Three

1. Clarence H. Danhof, *Government contracting and technological change.* Washington, D.C. The Brooking Institution: 1968, p. 1.

2. Rex Malik, "Europe moving to protect faltering DP industry," *Computerworld*, January 14, 1980, p. 12.

3. "European society faced with the challenge of new information technologies: A community response," Commission of the European Communities, COM (79) 650, Brussels, November 26, 1979, p. 7.

4. *Public Printing Reorganization Act of 1979*, Hearings, Committee on House Administration, House of Representatives, and the Committee on Rules and Administration, United State Senate, 96th Congress, 1st Session, on H.R. 4572 and S. 1436, July 10, 19, 24, & 26, 1979, Washington, D.C., p. 305.

5. Robert Reinhold, "Research by pentagon scheduled to receive fund increase of 21%," *The New York Times*, January 29, 1980, p. A1.

6. *Report to the Congress* by the Comptroller General of the United States, "Better information management policies needed: A study of scientific and bibilographic services," U.S. General Accounting Office, August 6, 1979, p. 1.

7. Circular No. A-76, revised, Office of Management and Budget, Executive Office of the President, Washington, D.C., March 29, 1979, emphasis added.

8. *Ibid.*

9. *Federal Government Printing and Publishing: Policy Issues*, Report of the Ad Hoc Advisory Committee on Revising Title 44 to the Joint Committee on Printing, U.S. Congress, U.S. GPO, Washington, D.C., p. 63.

10. Paul G. Zurkowski, "The information service environment: Relationships and priorities," paper for the National Commission on Libraries and Information Science, November 1974, Washington, D.C., pp. 5, 26.

11. Hearings, Public Printing Reorganization Act of 1979, pp. 257–258.

12. *Ibid.*

13. *Ibid.*

14. *Documents to the People*, Government Documents Roundtable, American Library Association, November 1979, *7* (6), p. 271, emphasis added.

15. David F. Noble & Nancy E. Pfund, "Business goes back to college," *The Nation*, September 20, 1980, p. 1.

16.   C. H. Danhof, *op. cit.*, pp. 7–9.

17.   Edward E. David, Jr., "Industrial research in America: Challenge of a new synthesis," *Science*, July 1980, *29*, (4), pp. 133–139.

18.   Jo Thomas, "Attempt to count U.S. consultants is called failure." *The New York Times*, October 15, 1979.

19.   *Documents to the People*, Government Documents Round Table, American Library Association, September 1980, *8* (5), p. 225.

20.   *Ibid.*

21.   *Federal Government Printing and Publishing: Policy Issues, op. cit.*, p. 44.

22.   Judith Miller, "Experts' advice on chrysler," *The New York Times*, September 17, 1979.

23.   *100 GPO years: 1861-1961, a history of United States public printing*, GPO, Washington, D.C., 1961.

24.   Congress of the United States, Joint Committee on Printing, Memorandum dated October 17, 1980, announcing open meetings in Los Angeles and San Francisco on the Federal Government's printing and distribution programs. From Augustus F. Hawkins, acting chairman of the Committee.

25.   *"Better information management needed: A study of scientific and technical bibliographic services, op. cit.*, Appendix VII, Report to the Congress by the Comptroller General of the U.S. Information Industry Association letter to Mr. J. H. Stolarow, Director, U.S. General Accounting Office, August 6, 1979, p. 56, emphasis added.

26.   Shawn P. Kelly, *The people's printer: A report on the Government Printing Office*, Washington, D.C., July 1979.

27.   *Ibid.*

28.   Sharon S. Gressle, *1978 Survey of selected publication practices of executive branch agencies*, The Library of Congress, Congressional Research Service, Washington, D.C., April 16, 1979, emphasis added.

29.   *Ibid.*

30.   *National Publications Act of 1980*, Report by the Committee on House Administration of the U.S. House of Representatives, 96th Congress, 2nd Session, House Report No. 96-836, Pt. 1, Washington, D.C., March 19, 1980, p. 21.

31.   Bertram Gross, *Friendly Fascism:* New York: E. Evans, 1980, p. 261.

32.   *Federal Register*, July 25, 1978, *43* (143), p. 32204–5.

33.   *Information Hotline*, Special Issue, March 1979, *11* (3).

34.   Office of Management and Budget, "Improved management and dissemination of Federal information: Request for comment," *Federal Register*, June 9, 1980, *45* (112), pp. 38461–38463.

35.   *Ibid.*, emphasis added.

36.   *Government Depository Libraries*, Revised April 1978, 95th Congress, 2nd Session, Joint Committee on Printing, Washington, D.C., p. 1.

37.   Even to obtain an index of the titles available from NTIS represents a sizable outlay, not easily managed by most depositories which have tightly limited budgets. An NTIS *Retrospective Index* for July 1964 through December 1978, for example, lists more than 750,000 publications and costs $600. A *Current Index*, which is a quarterly cumulation of new publications, costs $400 annually. The NTIS offers a "bargain" rate for the combined purchase of these indexes at $900. The fact that this important and expensive NTIS index did not come initially as a depository item created a furor in library circles. As a result, it eventually was made available by NTIS as a depository publication. *Documents to the People*, Government Round Table, American Library Association, September 1979, *7* (5), p. 182.

38.   Hearings, Public Printing Reorganization Act of 1979, *op. cit.*, pp. 260–261.

39.   *Ibid.*, p. 266.

40.   The National Publications Act of 1979, embodied in House Bill No. 5424, introduced into the House of Representatives on September 27, 1979, included section 707(a)2, which:
      provides that when public documents are made available to depository libraries under 707(a)1, the Director of Distribution Services (formerly, the Superintendent of Documents) shall provide the widest degree of choice both as to format—that is, paper, microform, online, etc.—and as to the source of such documents. For example, if the Director determines that it is more advantageous, cost-effective, useful or efficient to procure such documents from private commercial firms, then such sources may be utilized. *H.R. 5424*, National Publications Act of 1979, Print prepared for the Committee on House Administration, 96th Congress, 1st Session, U.S. GPO, Washington, D.C., October 1979, p. 14.

41.   President Carter, letter of transmittal for the Report of the White House Conference on Library and Information Services, The White House, September 26, 1980. Also, *LJ SLJ Hotline*, October 6, 1980, *9* (32), page IX–31.

42.   Deirde Carmody, "Measures to shield U.S. data criticized," *The New York Times*, May 4, 1980:

43.   Les Brown, "F.C.C.'s move to drop some radio rules," *The New York Times*, March 13, 1980, p. C22.

44.   Paul Zarins, University of California, San Diego Documents Librarian, in personal communication to the author.

45.   *Hearings* before the Subcommittee on Printing of the Committee

on House Administration, House of Representatives, 96th Congress, First Session, on H.R. 5424, The National Publicationss Act, November 14, 1979, U.S. GPO, Washington, D.C. Note the statements of these agencies in the Appendix of the Hearings.

46.   The White House Conference on Library and Information Services—179 Summary, March 1980, U.S., Washington, D.C. GPO See also, *Information World*, January 1980, p. 17.

47.   Tony Schwartz, "Corporations look to cable TV," *The New York Times*, October 18, 1980, p. 01.

48.   Phil Hirsch, "Groups demand stronger rewrite," *Computerworld*, January 21, 1980, pp. 1, 4.

49.   Edward E. David, Jr., "Industrial research in America: Challenge of a new synthesis," *Science*, July 4, 1980, *209*, pp. 133–139.

50.   Dr. Frank Press, Presidential Science Adviser, in *The New York Times*, by Robert Reinhold, "Research by Pentagon scheduled to receive fund increase of 21%," January 29, 1980, p. A1.

51.   "Harvard considers commerical role in DNA research," *The New York Times*, October 27, 1980. Also, David Noble & Nancy E. Pfund, "Business goes back to college," *op. cit.*

chapter four

Corporate Media:
The Appropriation of New
Communication Technologies
by the *Fortune 500*

We have the choice of resigning ourselves to reacting to the pressures and criticisms of others, or we can assume leadership roles and tell our story more effectively than ever before.

Leslie H. Warner, Chairman and Chief Executive Officer, GTE, in "Crosscurrents in corporate communications," Fortune, 1972.

'Issue Management' describes the process of integrating social and environmental trends into company planning and involving corporations in public policy formulation.

Merrill Rose, "Issues management and the consumer affairs professional," Public Relations Quarterly, Fall 1980, 25 (3).

While the privatization of newly generated information is accelerating, the process of corporate message making is also in the midst of a sweeping transformation. In the next chapter, the vital operational role that communication provides within the modern corporation, as well as its essential contribution to the entire world business system, will be examined. In this chapter, attention centers on the use of corporate media to influence national publics.

Business has never suffered for lack of access to the nations's informational and educational circuits. It has been provided ordinarily by outright ownership of presses and broadcasting facilities, institutionalized with financial support through advertising, and maintained unfailingly with decisive representation on administrative and decision-making bodies that ultimately approve the message and message transmitters.[1]

The mass communication technologies of the 20th century—film, radio, and television—have been utilized from their time of discovery for moneymaking and for the ideological indoctrination of their audiences. Corporate and systemic values have rarely been absent from the material transmitted—news or entertainment—though objectivity and value neutrality have been the customary claims of the transmitters.

In a totally new development, the latest communication technologies, such as video cassettes, home recorders, video discs, cable TV, computers, and direct satellite broadcasting, are providing corporations whose main economic activities are not in media production with remarkable opportunities to reach mass audiences directly with their messages. Reliance on the communication channels owned by established media interests can be reduced. The change this portends in the origin, character, diversity, and content of the messages that already are being, and will increasingly be, produced is momentous.

Individual super-corporations are beginning to reach out with their own professionally prepared media materials and messages, *without intermediaries*, to the national public.

One overriding corporate need and two other developments have come together recently to make direct, *general* corporate communications increasingly feasible and possible. The deepening socio-industrial crisis confronts corporate business with an ever increasing set of public questions and demands. At the same time, the development of the new communication technologies and the emergence of a supportive legal atmosphere for 'corporate speech' permit businesses to address national publics directly and effectively.

Coping with the problems of advanced capitalism is termed "issues management" by business. "Issues management" has risen to the top of the corporate daily agenda. A *Sloan Management Review* contributor indicates why this is so:

> As the 1970s come to a close, it is obvious to anyone involved with the private sector that severe management problems have grown up

around such areas as consumerism, environmental protection, occupational safety and health, and employment policy.[2]

In fact, it adds up to nothing less than a challenge to corporate legitimacy. "People will ask the question: "Is the market system serving us well?", and there will be an implicit willingness to discuss broad alternatives for reorganizing economic activity."

In fact, all of the American economy is open to such questioning: "The public is increasingly prepared to accept remedies to the oil crisis or a national gas crisis that, in either concept or effect, nationalizes the industry. With differences only in degree, similar prospects confront industries as diverse as insurance, communications, banking, electric power, food production, and transportation. Moreover, such a list is almost surely incomplete."

In sum, reaching the public effectively with the corporate viewpoint has become a fundamental requirement of modern business. "More than ever, people outside and inside the firm are recognizing that dealing with the corporation's external relations is the true frontier of modern management."

Yet while there is a greater need than ever for corporate perspectives to reach wide publics if the business system is to retain its legitimacy, the commercial media—the ordinary instruments for reaching these audiences—are not as dependable as business would like them to be. There are reasons for this. One is that the commercial informational system, if it is to continue to serve effectively general systemic and not merely sectoral or individual, corporate ends, requires credibility. Unexceptional one-dimensional programming soon would impair this crucial attribute.

A second condition which serves *sometimes* to circulate programming or informational material less than flattering to the corporate community is the commercial self-interest of the corporate media sector. Though this sector is no less private enterprise oriented than the rest of the *Fortune 500* contingent, its own profitability hinges on maintaining massive audience contact. This can be assured generally with thematic material—news or general programming—which stresses drama and tension, usually involving individuals and individual situations.

Despite the media's general avoidance of presenting the social basis of conflict situations, the directors and decision makers in the corporate hierarchies are not satisfied. It is their expectation that the social scene, individually and collectively, should appear without tension and conflict free.

Closely related to the programming factor, which affects media profitability, is the actual existence in the world, in the nation, and in the local community, of *real* conflict, tension, opposition, and resistance. Contrary to the image of basic social harmony that 'responsible' commentators in all the informational fields tirelessly seek to propagate, the divisions of income, race, sex, and age are present and exacerbated in the economy. Many would claim that they are becoming more intense all the time.

Abroad, the Third World nations press their claims for a greater share of global resources. At home, a half century of intense advertising has created a feeling of what some analysts call "entitlement:" the viewers and listeners want what they have been told in thousands of 'commercials' they 'need'. Accordingly, when an outburst of frustration, anger, or protest occurs, individually or collectively, media sometimes sees it as an opportunity for exploitation, as a money attracting potential.

Finally, one factor that can be exaggerated but which does exist in some measure, is the different outlooks between many of the workers in the informational industries and the corporate organizations in which they are employed. For some of the journalists, reporters, broadcasters, film-makers, artists, writers, editors, equipment operators, and other information makers and processors, corporate values leave much to be desired. Actually, many have been encouraged in their professional training to expose corruption and to act as the public's guardians. A goodly number of media workers, therefore, may be anti-monopoly and pro-environment, may espouse human capacity over technical efficiency, and may hold social well-being above private enrichment. To be sure, such views are customarily contained in the many checks and balances and stratifications that are carefully constructed in private and governmental bureaucracies. All the same, longstanding democratic ideals in the national heritage do retain influence and sometimes do collide with corporate perspectives.

For all the above and possibly other reasons, the information system which financially is at the disposition of the industrial oligarchy, seen from the corporate boardroom, is not without its deficiencies and unreliabilities. At times, it can even be viewed as an opposition.[3]

Rawleigh Warner, the chairman of the Mobil Oil corporation and a strong believer in communicating its views to the public, carefully expressed business' dissatisfaction with the mass media. In his criticism, Warner noted that the electronic media "are primarily in the business of entertainment and are structurally unable to handle complex issues well on their news shows."[4]

The Mobil chairman lists five reasons for the structural deficiency of network television news programs: (1) time limitations—fifteen or more items in 24 minutes of a daily national news—makes serious reportage impossible; (2) economic limitations—camera crews are expensive and can only be kept in a few places. This generally limits what viewers will see; (3) personalization of the news—"size of audiences becomes paramount, with the result that balanced presentation of the news is subordinated to personalities and showmanship"; (4) personnel limitations—other than for sports and weather, few specialists are used; and, (5) TV is an entertainment media—news therefore follows a show business or drama format, with conflict, problems, and revolution in the forefront."[5]

What these charges—all of them accurate—amount to is that Mobil Oil, and most if not all the other *Fortune 500* companies, are critical of media corporations' profit-making operations because they create informational and image problems for the subjects they cover.

It is a neat paradox. Media corporations, following profit maximizing principles common to all big business, aim for large audiences and attract them with sensational, conflictural, personalized, crisis-laden drama, both in the news and in the general programming. Yet the programming that makes money for CBS, ABC, NBC and other media conglomerates, may be acutely embarrassing and possibly damaging to the continued money-making operations of the rest of American corporate industry.

It is not by chance that it is a representative of an oil company who is most scathing in denouncing electronic journalism. The oil 'crisis', soaring gasoline prices, Middle East politics, environmental pollution, the collapse of the American car industry, and so on, constitute an inescapable reality which cannot be passed over by information managers, were they willing to do so.

They are not willing to drop it entirely because it provides drama, villains, and heroes, the stuff that pulls in mass audiences.

Given these conditions, it is no wonder that the oil companies are not ecstatic about the coverage their role in the energy field receives. Seen from a truly social standpoint, the oil corporations are getting off fairly well—much better than the situation or their behavior demand. Serious, critical, continuing coverage would make it literally impossible for them to maintain their general economic-political policies, to say nothing of their outlandish profits of the last several years.

Other examples are too numerous to mention. One, in particular, points up the general dilemma for the corporate community. The frightful human costs of the seepage of chemical wastes in the New York State Love Canal community have received national media coverage for the human interest and community distress characteristics of the story. It is an outcome of years of careless, if not criminal, dumping of toxic chemicals by a major chemical company, now a subsidiary of a still larger oil corporation. These practices have not sat well with the TV viewers of the nation. Similarly the Metropolitan Utility Corporation, as well as other utility companies, are not singing the praises of the national media for their coverage of Three Mile Island and other nuclear near-miss disasters.

In these episodes of corporate malfeasance, the profit-making interests of the media collide with those of the nonmedia *Fortune 500*. Mobil Oil's Warner does not fail to see this:

> The irony lies in the obvious fact that the 'press' is itself a business, with the need to earn a profit or go under . . . so it becomes urgent that both business and the media heal the breach between them and find ways to achieve certain common goals in the public interest.[6]

What is being suggested here, most discreetly, is that the common interest, not of the public, as Warner disingenuously puts it, but of the corporate sector, be put above the profits of the corporate media component. Operating in public forums, code words such as the "social responsibility" of the media are invoked to persuade the information conglomerates to respect the overall interest of the dominant class, while not alerting the population in general to the coercion that is occurring.

Much of the same theme is taken up in a report prepared for the Trilateral Commission, the body which attempts to reconcile not

only national ruling class conflicts but also the international rivalries of Western Europe, Japanese, and United States capitalism:

> The increase in media power is not unlike the rise of the industrial
> corporation to national power at the end of the nineteenth century.
> Just as the corporations enveloped themselves in the constitutional
> protection of the due process clause, the media now defend them-
> selves in terms of the First Amendment. In both cases, there obvi-
> ously are important rights to be protected, *but broader interests of
> society and government are also at stake.* In due course, beginning
> with the Interstate Commerce Act and the Sherman Anti-trust Act,
> measures had to be taken to regulate the new industrial centers of
> power and to define their relations to the rest of society. *Something
> comparable appears to be now needed with respect to the media.*[7]

Corporate royalty is giving the media barons fair warning. Shape
up or be confined by royal criteria of "social responsibility."

As the financial editor of *The New York Times* observed, the
Trilaterial Commission's historical analogy, which cited the effort
to "regulate the new industrial centers of power" in America at the
end of the 19th century, with a call today to do the same with the
media, is false.[8]

The early efforts arose out of popular, mass indignation against
the trusts and monopolies. The current drive to reduce the authority of the media comes not from the people but from the elite itself,
upset with even partial and quite limited information made available about the various crises that are shaking the global and national
equilibria.

One means, then, of the dominant corporate interest to obtain
still further control of the country's informational climate—
acknowledging their already preponderant position—is to press for
legislative, judicial, or legal measures that will hold the media still
more accountable to the ruling power centers.

An obstacle to early accomplishment of this objective is the First
Amendment, which media combines are neither slow nor reluctant
to call upon. The national democratic tradition, therefore, makes
the "socially accountable" course to coerce the media uncertain. It
becomes risky if it in any way appears to threaten another vital part
of the still influential American ideology—the espousal, at least
formalistically, of free speech.

The corporate business system's need for a protective and supportive informational environment grows more pressing, but obtaining it from the commercial mass media remains problematic. Two new developments seem to offer a way out of this corporate bind. Together they permit massive message making of corporate programming directly deliverable to people everywhere.

TWO PRE-CONDITIONS OF DIRECT CORPORATE COMMUNICATION WITH NATIONAL PUBLICS

The *new communication technology* is the material basis upon which the new option of direct corporate communications rests. The range of electronic instrumentation now available, and the transmission systems in place or being organized, permit those with the economic resources to have communication systems custom made to their needs and specifications.

Portable recording equipment, video discs, video cassettes, home recorders and playback machines, computers, cable TV, and satellite transmission can be put together in highly specific combinations to allow individual messages to be produced and transmitted to large and growing numbers of listeners and viewers, *in their homes and in their places of work*, across the country and around the world.

The second prerequisite for corporate message making and dissemination on an altogether new scale and intensity is a supportive legal framework. This too now exists. Corporate communications directly to the public, paid for out of corporate revenues derived from the public, have received unprecedented legal legitimation in recent Supreme Court decisions.[9]

In 1978 the Supreme Court, in a five to four decision, affirmed the right of a private corporation to spend money to publicize its views. In this instance it was to oppose a referendum to amend the Massachusetts Constitution to authorize the legislature to enact a graduated income tax. This has become known as the *Bellotti* decision.

With this decision, the corporation, long regarded by judicial interpretation as an individual, was granted broad First Amendment rights of paid free speech. The thinking of the Court on this issue is instructive. Writing for the majority, Justice Powell saw no difference in quality or impact between the speech of an individual and that of a giant company. He said that free speech

> Is indispensable to decision-making in a democracy, and this is no less true because speech comes from a corporation rather than an individual . . . The inherent worth of speech in terms of its capacity for informing the public does not depend upon the identity of its source, whether a corporation, association, union, or individual.

Chief Justice Burger, in a concurring opinion, was more cognizant of the existing structure of information power. He noted that those who now carry on the "business of communications" are likely to be "large media conglomerates" engaged in a variety of informational activities, horizontally as well as vertically. When organized, these media businesses, Burger suggested, might pose "a much more realistic threat to valid interests" in "shaping popular opinion on public issues." As media conglomerates now constitute the informational environment, why not allow nonmedia corporations also to have full rights of expression? Burger asked.

Justice White, writing for the minority, dealt directly with the essential issue. Is corporate speech the same as individual expression? "Indeed," he observed, "what some have considered to be the principal function of the First Amendment, the use of communication as a means of self-expression, self-realization and self-fulfillment, is not at all furthered by corporate speech. It is clear that the communication of profitmaking corporations are not 'an integral part of the development of ideas, mental exploration and of the affirmation of self'. They do not represent a manifestation of individual freedom or choice."

Justice White concluded, "corporate expenditures designed to further political causes lack the connection with individual self-expression which is one of the principal justifications for the constitutional protection of speech provided by the First Amendment."[10]

In June 1980, the Supreme Court again considered the issue of corporate expression. Again, it ruled in two cases in favor of a "major expansion of the free speech rights of corporations."[11] In one case, the Court accepted the right of utility corporations to insert into monthly bills statements of their positions on "continual matters of public policy." In the second case, the Court ruled against the New York State Public Service Commission, which had

issued a ban on advertising by utility corporations seeking to promote the use of electricity.

These Court decisions (*Bellotti* in 1978 and *Con Edison* in 1980)
came at a very propitious time for the launching of corporate
messages directly to the American public. It is a juncture well described by William Read as "The First Amendment Meets the
Second Revolution," the second revolution meaning the new communication technology that has become available for expanded
message making and dissemination. "The ability to communicate to
masses of people," Read observed, "is spreading beyond 'the institutional media'. "[12]

This ability, however, is not evenly distributed throughout the
society. Though hypothetically available to individual and business
alike, the national reality of unequal resource command allows only
certain very privileged groups and entities to "communicate to
masses of people." These are, for the most part, the *Fortune 500*
folk.

One of the inner ring of this very special circle of interests, the
Chase Manhattan Bank, claiming the First Amendment as its heritage, announced boldly that "We'll continue to speak out, in accordance with the wishes of our Founding Fathers."[13]

CORPORATE APPROPRIATION OF THE NEW COMMUNICATION TECHNOLOGY

At the end of the 1970s a vice president of the Committee for
Economic Development, a business public policy grouping, observed that "with the explosion of media technology, American corporations are entering a new world." In this new world, he found
that "some three hundred United States firms whose principal business is outside of the media have developed a major video capacity
for in-house corporate newscasts—some with film, video-tape, and
computerized editing facilities that rival those of the national networks."[14]

These facilities are not gathering dust. In 1977, it was estimated
that "U.S. business and non-profit organizations [would] produce
more television programming for their own internal use than will
have been carried by ABC, CBS, NBC and PBS combined."[15]

It is a rapidly changing corporate communications environment.
Each inventory of the private industrial use of video and film re-

veals increased installation of facilities and their utilization. In the second of the two most comprehensive surveys of the nonbroadcast private television industry by Judith M. Brush and Douglas P. Brush, in 1977, these developments are reported:

1.   "More than 700 organizations will produce over 46,000 video programs totalling some 15000 hours by the end of the year."
2.   Almost half (47.3%) of the user organizations have more than 10,000 employees.
3.   More than two-thirds of the study's respondents have video networks ("a user-originated distribution system which carries user-originated program material to six or more locations away from the point of origination"). The authors estimate that as of 1977, "there are now at least 200 private video networks with more than 20 locations."
4.   Video-cassettes are the chief form of program distribution. Three-quarters of the surveyed organizations use them.[16]

It seems certain that the private, nonbroadcast, video industry has grown significantly in the last few years and that the survey figures given above greatly understate the current dimensions of the field.

Precisely because private video communications are so recent and their uses expanding so rapidly, it would be premature to come to definite judgments about the ultimate meaning and impact of this new communication development. It is still a very experimental area. Many companies report, and the evidence demonstrates, continuously expanding uses for the private systems. The primary uses in the future, therefore, may differ considerably from those that are presently dominant. The discussion that follows must be understood in this light. It can only be suggestive of certain likely developments on the basis of trends already manifest.

Private television is already a major phenomenon, "an awakening giant" in the words of the survey-takers. The findings indicate that the major users, as could be anticipated, are the largest corporations in the country. The existence in 1977 of over 200 private networks with more than 20 locations confirms the already strong presence of the *Fortune 500* in corporate video.

This being so, the *audiences* for the in-house programming, though not subject yet to Nielsen ratings—a development yet to come—already must be counted in upwards of six figures. And far more significant for the future are the extra-corporate audiences, the publics not in the company's work force.

THE USES OF CORPORATE VIDEO

The uses of corporate video have evolved rapidly. In the first few years, emphasis was mostly on safety, product use, and employee training all of which remain important subjects for in-house programming. Dupont, for example, "has a library of 700 training tapes designed for in-house use." Union Carbide in 1979, "produced 385 programs, of which 60–65 were training programs."[17]

Private television, according to the Brushes, "started in most organizations in the training department." It has quickly become a management medium, "communicating corporate goals and other policy statements to a large and varied work force located around the country and possibly around the world."[18] Repeatedly, in accounts of company utilization of in-house video, TV is found to be "a very credible source of information . . . [which can be] designed to appeal to a younger, sometimes suspicious work force."[19]

The effectiveness and credibility of the electronic image made it inevitable that an expanding number of applications and uses would be discovered by imaginative producers and administrators. They have. Though the field is still in its enfancy, already some developments give a sense of what may be expected in a very short time. Bank of America, for example, produces "Video Bankamerican," which is distributed to 1200 domestic and 110 overseas branches. It is designed to "inform employees of new policies and procedures, and bring a sense of togetherness." The 1300 viewing locations have a potential audience of 80,000. Dow Chemical's division in Midland, Michigan, has been producing a corporate weekly report for almost five years. The company has 300 TV receivers on-line internally. Programs are also aired on public cablevision, feeding homes in four cities with a potential audience of 25,000.[20]

Another example of corporate video use extending well beyond the training sphere, but still confined to the in-house work force, is company closed circuit television during union organizing campaigns. The vice president of industrial relations of Florida Steel Corporation offers a description and evaluation of his company's successful effort, utilizing closed-circuit TV, to block the United Steel Workers' organizing efforts at three Tampa company locations. These points are made: (1) television is the most dramatic and therefore effective medium to stating management's case; (2) present TV technology is remarkably flexible and simple and can be used easily in factory or office, away from commercial studies; (3) sophisticated and skilled TV workers, technicians, and creative personnel, are relatively available on a freelance basis, especially if the location is near a metropolitan area; (4) the company should use TV *before* the union's organizational effort begins, so the workers do not feel that the anti-union programming is a one-time, special effort, directed exclusively against organization; (5) television is most effective if it is used along with and in support of traditional and familiar communications—mailings, leaflets, posters, telephone programs, and personal contact; (6) employees should not be forced to watch the company program on their own time—paid company time makes the material more palatable; (7) "third person," non-company personnel, announcers, and reporters, provide more credibility to the company program; "newscasts must avoid taking a totally subjective company line if credibility is to be maintained"; (8) the program has to be done well ("professionally") to be effective.[21]

The author of this account emphasizes that the anti-union programming is important but still only one episode in the company's *ongoing* communication program. Already, many companies are producing materials for regular, continuing, viewing schedules. The manager of programs for the General Telephone Company of Florida (GT/F), described a packet of regularly appearing programs his company produces: a several-year-old TV news program for management and hourly employees; a monthly informational program, 20 minutes in length with subjects ranging from legislation to new products and services; and "political awareness programs [which] have been produced in every election year since 1972." Indicative of the kind of awareness created, the company's program series "Election '74" won a Freedom Foundations Award, an ultraconservative acknowledgement.

The GT/F program manager noted that most company in-house TV facilities were acquired originally on the basis of their training potential. This view is now changing. "More corporate TV professionals now realize that the prime objective of every program is to teach or to inform, or possibly both."[22]

Still another corporate communications manager—for Union Carbide Corporation—elaborates on this. "As we now know," he writes, "video is not solely a training nor an employee communication tool. It is a training and an employee communication tool, and a management/communication tool, and a sales promotion tool, and a tool of recruiting, security analyst relations, community relations, and so on."[23] This realization is at the base of the constantly widening sphere of corporate video communication. Once the full potential of video message making is recognized and its enormous credibility demonstrated, why should it be limited to in-house employee audiences, large as they might be? Why, indeed?

The Union Carbide Corporation video communication manager asked the same question and allowed his imagination to run a few years ahead. Writing a futuristic memorandum to his superior, the Vice President of Corporate Communications, he states:

> today [December 1, 1983] corporate executives not only see their role differently than they did in the mid-'70's, but also they have a better appreciation of the need for communication with audiences *inside and outside the company*, as well as the communications process itself.[24]

The audiences "outside" could be "governments, consumer groups, environmentalists, foreign competition and employees"[25]—in short, the world at large.

For a rapidly growing number of corporations, this is not a distant prospect; it is already happening. Efforts of private companies to have their views and perspectives directly presented to specific or even national audiences are increasingly observable, though still mostly in print form. In some localities, utility company views are distributed with monthly billing statements. Yet this, too, may be changing.

Atlantic Richfield and Refining Co. (ARCO), one of the oil 'majors', "doesn't like the way it's depicted on television," *The Wall Street Journal* reports. Unlike most dissatisfied viewers, ARCO can do something about it. "For the past year," the *Journal* notes, "ARCO has been producing a slick, half-hour 'news magazine' called 'Energy Update', once a month." Professionally done and, at first glance, a balanced presentation, the program is sent free to "139 domestic and foreign stations, including 106 commercial and public broadcasting channels and 24 cable operations in the U.S."[26]

Anthony P. Hatch, ARCO's manager of media relations, says, "We don't care if ARCO isn't given credit," when only segments of the programs are used by some stations.[27] The huge and continuous programming needs of television make such professionally prepared material, especially when it is available free of charge, highly attractive to many commercial station owners and managers.

In another instance, in December 1979, a utility company video program was produced to refute a CBS "60 Minutes" segment in which the company perceived itself to be treated unfairly. Illinois Power Company did not deliberately plan for a national distribution of its own 42 minute video answer to "60 Minutes." It originally sent the tapes to employees, customers, shareholders, and the investment community. The interest in Illinois Power's use of television as a format for reply was so intense that more than 2000 copies were distributed "for showings by corporations, trade associations, journalism schools and community organizations."[28] The company concluded that "as a means of reaching the thinking people and thoughtshapers, this is just an excellent medium."[29] Kaiser Aluminum and Chemical Corporation went a step further in its manner of reply to an ABC news magazine "20/20" program segment that it found objectionable. Kaiser insisted that ABC carry an unedited video response of a four-minute rebuttal it prepared itself. This airing of a non-network-produced response, "which no network seems ever to have done before," many electronic journalists "view as a demoralizing precedent."[30]

It is demoralizing not so much because the network monopoly over program production is breached. Ordinarily this could be regarded as a welcome broadening of the spectrum of opinion. However, resource realities and the distribution of power in the United States do not permit such an optimistic assessment. The problem is that the corporate giants, not the general public, have the resources, the facilities, and the hired expertise to produce video presentations of their views.

Fortune 500 companies are not losing much time in expressing themselves publicly. Mobil Oil's chairman, Rawleigh Warner, referring to all kinds of corporate communications, puts it this way: "In our view, we have no practical alternative to speaking up publicly. We think it is no exaggeration to say we have to publish or perish, and we do not intend to perish if we can help it."[31]

Far from perishing, Mobil has produced eleven televised special reports on energy issues since 1976. Sixty-two TV stations have shown Mobil's 1980 special report, "Energy At The Crossroads." Commenting on this activity, *Los Angeles Times'* business reporter, A. Kent MacDougall observed: " "Energy At the Crossroads' is as notable for what it leaves out as for what it includes. For one thing, there is no hint that the seemingly neutral interviews were conducted by a Mobil retainer."[32]

Saturating media channels with corporate messages is, of course, no recent development. Newspapers and magazines for decades have been filled with corporate PR, presented as "news" and noteworthy articles. Now a genuinely new situation appears to be developing. Though commercial media channels, especially TV, continue to be used to disseminate corporate perspectives in programs often produced by the companies themselves, the big corporations, by employing the new communication technologies, can electronically 'publish' their points of view and directly transmit them to national and global audiences.

Home and office video recorders and playback equipment have been available and purchased in growing volume in recent years. Now video discs and video disc playback machines are about to be launched on an extensive scale, enabling consumers, employees, homes, and offices to view video programs made from whatever source.[33] Who, if not the *Fortune 500*, are better prepared to provide video cassettes and discs for these ever more numerous recording and playback machines?

The full impact of nonmedia corporate communications, directed to general audiences, remains to be seen and felt, but one conclusion cannot be avoided. All the technological and financial resources that the *Fortune 500* can assemble to present their interpretations of the issues and crises affecting American life cannot insure popular acceptance. Credibility remains a major consideration.

ARCO's manager of media relations is very sensitive to this problem. "Credibility is an issue . . . . If we slip just once by avoiding a tough question or ignoring the other side, then we rightfully deserve to be ignored."[34] Perhaps this is company policy. It remains to be seen.

Other company communication managers are equally concerned. For this reason, the use of "third person," non-company personnel, announcers, and reporters, is preferred. It is considered to bestow more credibility on company programs. Wide use already is being made of recognizable commercial broadcasters who are presented as nonpartisan. Mobil Oil, for example, has a stable of "half a dozen reporters who have placed their credibility as objective journalists in Mobil's service."[35]

But while direct corporate communications may be restrained somewhat by the credibility factor, the commercial media are seemingly becoming more solicitous of business views, while they observe corporate watchdogs scrutinizing every move they make. The net effect of these developments probably will be a convergence, leading to low-keyed, highly professional presentations of business perspectives and values. These will saturate increasingly the national communication atmosphere, the customary media channels, and the new, direct, nonmedia corporate communications alike.

Where will independent journalism and journalists find themselves in this convergence? Indeed, where will the national public go to get differing outlooks and perspectives? These are the forgotten but basic questions in what is solemnly called "the information age."

Notes to Chapter Four

1. Peter Dreier & Steve Weinberg, "Interlocking directorates," *Columbia Journalism Review*, November/December 1979, pp. 51–68.

2. James E. Post, "The corporation in the public policy process—A view toward the 1980s," *Sloan Management Review*, Forum, Fall 1979, pp. 45–52.
    Also see, S. Prakash Sethi, *Advocacy advertising and large Corporations*. Lexington, Mass. D.C. Heath & Co.: 1977.

3. "Business and the media," *Dun's Review*, May 1977, *109* (5), p. 76.

4. Rawleigh Warner, Jr. & Leonard S. Silk, *Ideals in collision: The relationship between business and the news media*, Carnegie Mellon University Press, distributed by Columbia University Press, New York, 1979, pp. 29-30.

5. *Ibid.*, p. 30.

6. *Ibid.*, p. 36.

7. *The Crisis of Democracy*, Report on the Governability of Democracies to the Trilateral Commission. New York: New York University Press, 1977, pp. 99–100, emphasis added. (Quoted in Warner & Silk, *op. cit.*)

8. Warner & Silk, *op. cit.*, p. 55.

9. *First National Bank of Boston et al.* v. *Bellotti, Attorney General of Mass. et al.*, and *Central Hudson Gas* v. *Public Service Commission*, June 20, 1980.

10.   *Bellotti, op. cit.*

11.   Linda Greenhouse, "Two rulings by High Court expand corpora-
      tions' free speech rights," *The New York Times*, June 21, 1980, p.
      1.

12.   William H. Read, "The First Amendment meets the Second Revo-
      lution", Working Paper W-79-3, Program on Information Re-
      sources Policy, Harvard University, Cambridge, Mass., March
      1979.

13.   *The New York Times*, July 24, 1980, full page advertisement, p.
      D3.

14.   Sol. Hurwitz, "On the road to wired city," *Harvard Magazine*,
      September/October 1979, pp. 18–19.

15.   Judith M. Brush & Douglas P. Brush, "Corporate video: Bur-
      geoning role for PR," *Public Relations Journal*, October 1977, *33*
      (10), p. 14.

16.   Judith M. Brush & Douglas P. Brush, *Private television commu-
      nications: An awakening giant.* Boston, Mass.: Herman Pub-
      lishing, Inc., 1977.

17.   "Industrial training goes big-league," *Chemical Weekly*, May 21,
      1980, p. 48.

18.   Judith M. Brush & Douglas P. Brush, *Private television commu-
      nications, op. cit.*, pp. 11–12.

19.   Frank L. Riggs, "Turning employees on with TV," *Public Rela-
      tions Journal*, February 1980, p. 23.

20.   ITVA Survey Sheets are part of the TV News Producers Profile
      file, compiled by ITVA member Edward S. Wyatt (Du Pont). Cop-
      ies were forwarded to ITVA member Dan Sullivan, University of
      California, San Diego Media Center, upon request.

21.   James C. Hogue, "Using closed-circuit television during union
      organizing campaigns," *Personnel*, September/October 1977, pp.
      72–75.

22.   Billy Bowes, "Private TV: Building corporate credibility," *Public
      Relations Journal*, September 1978, *34*, (9), pp. 36–37.

23.   Eugene Marlow, "The future of corporate video," *Industrial Mar-
      keting*, December 1978, pp. 51–54, emphasis added.

24.   *Ibid.*, emphasis added.

25.   *Ibid.*

26.   Stephen J. Sansweet, "ARCO TV show combats 'bias' of news-
      casts," *The Wall Street Journal*, August 1, 1980, p. 1.

27.   A Kent MacDougall, "Business increasingly uses (in both senses)
      media to push views," *The Los Angeles Times*, November 16,
      1980.

28.   *Ibid.*

29. Sandy Graham, "Illinois power pans '60 Minutes' ", *Wall Street Journal*, June 27, 1980.

30. John E. Cooney, "ABC agrees to air a rebuttal by Kaiser to '20/20' charges," *The Wall Street Journal*, November 3, 1980.

31. Warner & Silk, *op. cit.*, p. 23.

32. A. Kent MacDougall, *op. cit.*

33. "Video discs: A three-way race for a billion dollar jackpot," *Business Week*, July 7, 1980, pp. 72–82

34. Stephen J. Sansweet, *op. cit.*

35. A. Kent MacDougall, *op. cit.*

chapter five

The *Fortune 500* and the International Flow of Information: Transborder Data Flows and the Global Integration of the World Business System

When defined in the broadest possible sense, the subject of international data flows, although not yet widely recognized as such, could be one of the paramount issues in the closing years of the 20th century. Technology transfer, cultural dominance, industrial strength, full employment, mass education are only a few of the issues lying beneath the surface.[1]

William L. Fishman, formerly Assistant Director for International Communications, Office of Teleconmmunications Policy, Executive Office of the President; now, Senior Policy Advisor, National Telecommunication Information Agency

Advanced communication technology is offering corporate business new opportunities for profit making domestically and, no less important, for disseminating its ideology more effectively. At the same time, the new instrumentation has become indispensable to the global activities of the *Fortune 500*.

How rapidly the international information system is being transformed into a still more powerful infrastructure of domination and control may be appreciated by examining briefly a vital application of computer and satellite communications technology: transnational border data flows. The development and the application of a new technology are themselves lessons in the exercise of power. They reveal which elements in the social order are able to produce and direct the technology to what ends. With this in mind, analysis of the emerging system of international electronic communications provides a means of understanding who will be exercising decision-making power in the international order in the last decades of the 20th century.

The world economy, directed by transnational corporations (TNCs), that has developed since the end of the Second World War would be unimaginable without the tremendous changes in communication technology resulting from the use of satellites, computers, microwave transmission, cable networks, and television. Actually, the relationship is interactive. The giant companies that have taken over large chunks of global production and distribution[2] rely completely on an informational infrastructure which permits them to transmit and receive, almost instantaneously, billions of bits of data essential to the daily management of their global economic operations. Without this information, the routine business of the TNCs would be inconceivable. Equally significant in the long run is the heavy dependence otherwise powerful organizations have on uninterrupted information flows.

At the same time, the technology which facilitates these operations continues to be invented and developed, largely to serve the very special needs of companies with facilities around the world as well as the military machine which protects these activities. It is the military structure, and to a much lesser extent the super-corporations, which finance the research and development costs on which the technology is ultimately dependent. Actually, it has been the State—the United States Government—which has underwritten the R & D costs of the advanced communications technology. The government circuits through which the expenditures have been channelled are NASA and DOD.[3] The Department of Defense, for example, has spent about two billion dollars on laser research in recent years, in the expectation of producing, among other benefits, a death ray.[4]

The management of the world economy by a few thousand transnational corporations, two-thirds of which are owned by U.S. private interests, is reflected in the massive growth of information flows across national borders—flows which enable the companies to transact their global business and further integrate the internationalization of capital. Seemingly only exchanges of business data, these transnational data flows constitute the central nervous system of the transnational corporate system. Raw material stocks, production schedules, quality control, personnel records, tax and legal information, currency transactions, profit repatriation, and investment decisions are some of the constituents of a continuously swelling volume of data flows circulating *inside* transnational corporate business structures *across* national boundaries.

Yet despite their central importance, it is remarkable how limited the actual knowledge about transborder data flows is. No one presently knows the volume of data actually moving across borders, though some studies are being undertaken to provide at least limited answers.[5] Actually, the absence of solid statistical data derives directly from the private, intra-corporate nature of most of the transnational border data flows. According to a former State Department adviser on these matters, "the companies' worries over protecting corporate secrets [are] stronger than their desire to supply the information."[6] It is recognized, however, that although there is already a huge volume of such flows, it is produced by less than one-third of the world's countries.[7]

The types of flows too, though not yet specified precisely, can be fairly well identified. The TNCs, as could be expected, are the source of a large, if not the major, portion of the data traffic. Canada's Deputy Minister of Communications, Bernard Ostry, stated in 1980 that "90% of the flows with which we and others in the world are concerned, result from the inhouse activities of multinational organizations, and do not relate to services purchased on the free market."[8] Substantiation of this estimate is found in the "giant SITA network of international airlines [which] carried some 100,000 million characters of traffic a year . . . [and] a good many of the world's multinational companies have networks carrying in the order of 1,000 million to 10,000 or 20,000 million characters a year."[9]

The executive vice president of *Citibank*, the second largest commercial bank in the United States, with more than 200 branches overseas, explained the enormous needs of his bank and the few dozen other banks engaged in worldwide finance. He described

Globecom, "a private, automated global communications network" with lines that interconnect 80 of the bank's overseas branches in 65 countries. In 1977 he noted, "Today *Globecom* handles about 325,000 transmissions per month." Besides, "Citibank is also planning to link to another privately leased international network known as SWIFT. SWIFT stands for the society for worldwide interbank financial telecommunications. Its members include about 500 European, Canadian, and U.S. banks in 15 countries."[10] By 1980, bank membership had increased to about 750 banks in 27 countries.[11]

Illustrative of the general TNC dependence on computer communications is the example of Texas Instruments Company, a U.S. TNC engaged in the manufacture of advanced communications technology. "TI has 47 plants in 19 countries, and at any one of them a manager can plug into a worldwide communications system to see how he's doing and how he should be doing. It is all on record in a large computer in Dallas."[12]

Is it any wonder, when governmental policy on transborder data flows is being formulated, that the State Department goes directly to those most concerned and involved with these flows? The Bulletin of the American Society for Information Science reports that "The State Department has recently solicited information from some 140 chairmen of the boards of the 'largest companies' to assess the economic impact of transborder data flow restrictions on multinational corporations."[13]

It is apparent that international data flows are of great *and growing* importance to the operation and maintenance of the TNC world business system. The capability of TNCs to utilize productive facilities where the costs are lowest and the profits highest, to penetrate markets with massive advertising campaigns, to avoid or minimize taxes by shifting production, and to take advantage of fluctuating currencies by transferring funds from one center to another, is almost totally dependent on secure and instantaneous global communications.

For example, the unsettled international financial market is a source of both profitmaking and anxiety for the world banking system. Money can be made from instability as well as security. The Federal Reserve Bank of New York reported that "foreign exchange trading in the United States has grown almost five-fold since 1977. . . . Gross currency transactions by United States banks. . .averaged $23.4 billion on each business day in March, 1980, ecompared with an average of $5.3 billion a day in April, 1977.[14] Thus, it should be abundantly clear that the active and expanding private international networks of communications being utilized by the TNCs are a means of enormous power for the world business system, while at the same time they are a worrisome point of vulnerability.

How this power may be exercised is the next question to be considered. It should be emphasized however, that the character and the content of the vast bulk of the data flowing across national boundaries is private, circulating inside corporate organizations, and consequently beyond public scrutiny or even awareness. This lack of knowledgeability makes it all the more difficult to analyze precisely the impact of these flows. What follows, therefore, must of necessity be a somewhat speculative reconstruction.

ACCOUNTABILITY AND NATIONAL RESPONSIBILITY

If we take two known features of the contemporary international economy and relate them to transnational data flows, a remarkable, and shadowy transactional world becomes dimly visible.

Mention has been made of the SWIFT network, linking scores of the largest banks in the world. Noted also were intra-bank, private data processing and transmission networks, e.g., Citibanks's Globecom. At the same time as these informational networks have been established, another phenomenon has grown up in the world economy, what *Business Week* calls "stateless money"—"a vast, integrated global money and capital system, *almost totally outside all governmental regulation*, that can send billions of Euro-dollars, Euromarks, and other 'stateless' currencies hurtling around the world 24 hours a day." And this is no idle possibility. In fact, "huge amounts of these Eurocurrencies have leaked across national boundaries and out of government hands."

Who are responsible for the existence and use of this vast pool of stateless money, now estimated to range from $500 billion to a trillion dollars? Again, *Business Week* informs us that "of all the forces responsible for the creation and expansion of the free Euromarkets and the pool of stateless money, none has been as powerful as the

need of the 450 biggest multinational corporations in the world."
The magazine reports further that "now international commerce is
totally dependent on the new supranational banking system." Still
more significant, "the world of stateless money has in turn bred a
stateless banking system in which national boundaries mean very
little. Though Citicorp has its headquarters in New York City, the
institution today operates in dozens of countries . . . its World Corporation group was set up in 1974 to provide global banking services to global multinationals in any currency in any country."

What allows this world-wide system to function? *Business Week*
states that "tying together the vast new supranational banking system is a technology that has outpaced not only the ability of nations
to deal with it but even the perception by government officials that
a new bank order has been created. A computerized system links
banks around the world, allowing them to buy and sell deposits in a
unified global money market and to make loans anywhere and
anytime."

The combination of unregulated pools of capital and unregulated
data flows which direct the utilization of this capital make national
decision making increasingly problematic, even for the most powerful nations. *Business Week* observes that "when stateless money
moves against the currencies of the central banks, the outcome is
obvious . . . multinational   corporations   routinely   use   the
Euromarkets to finance their operations at the lowest possible cost,
and that often means making end runs around foreign policies. Last
year (for example), Olin Corporation saved a lot of money by using
Euro-Belgian francs to finance its Italian Subsidiary. In this case,
the Euromarkets provided a cheap, efficient source of financing to
the U.S. multinational. *But it did by-pass Italian monetary policy
that was aimed at lowering inflation by raising interest rates*".[15]

Mr. Will Sparks, a vice president of *Citibank*, observed how corporations in the United States in 1980 also are circumventing their
Government's anti-inflation policy. "There is a new burst of innovative financing now going on," Sparks notes, "in which U.S.
companies are arranging loans abroad unavailable to them at
home . . . once again, a national government trying to cope with
economic problems at home is stimulating new activity in the stateless marketplace." According to this international banker, "what all
this adds up to, is another profound challenge to the unlimited sov-

ereign power of nation-states brought about by the technical realities of global communications."[16] Neatly omitted from this analysis is the sovereign power of the TNCs, who created and exploit the "stateless marketplace."

These activities, it should be remembered, are occurring in developed, rich, and sophisticated (in a market-financial sense) West European and North American locales. Imagine the field for maneuver the TNCs enjoy in the poor, less developed societies with their weaker infrastructures!

Supranational electronic data flows, facilitating the almost-instantaneous transfer of huge pools of supranational capital, constitute but one, admittedly powerful, combination which undermines national sovereignty for the benefit of the TNCs. Equally elusive to national oversight are the policy decisions of TNCs with respect to investment, production, market pricing, sales, taxes, profits, depreciation and related matters. Here too, the utilization of private electronic data processing and transmission makes it possible for national policy in any of these areas to be circumvented relatively easily by firms operating in several countries but centrally directing their strategies.

These areas of corporate decision making and communications remain almost totally screened from public monitoring. Occasionally, some individual transgression inadvertently gets picked up, but if this does occur, full knowledgability remains unavailable because of the sorry state of TNC accounting standards and procedures. The question of standardizing accounting methods of transnational corporations has been a subject of attention by UN special committees for some time. Though efforts continue to try to introduce some compatibility and minimal criteria of record keeping, ultimate control of the books continues to reside deep in the financial recesses of TNC corporate structure. [17]

In fact, a good share of the accounting of TNC books is done by a few, mostly American, multinational accounting enterprises such as Peat, Marwick, Mitchell; Arthur Anderson; Price Waterhouse; Coopers and Lybrand; etc. It is stretching trust to its thinnest to rely on an "accounting ethic" to transcend powerful mutualities of interests.

The relatively uncomplicated side of corporate secrecy—the capability for hidden pay-offs, e.g., CIA affiliations—surfaces occasionally and briefly to public view.[18] The daily, operational decisions of the controllers of a good share of global economic activity go unscrutinized, facilitated by electronic networks.

COMPUTER COMMUNICATIONS, TRANSBORDER DATA FLOW, AND NATIONAL SECURITY

Computer communications and the transborder data flows they facilitate are now indispensable to the operation and maintenance of a world economy dominated by TNCs. Yet the ability of American companies to operate on a global scale and enjoy the benefits of worldwide resource and market exploitation would be unimaginable without the full backup of a concentrated military power, ready for instantaneous deployment and intervention. The alert system for this infrastructure of intervention relies on "27 major U.S. military command posts around the world. The computers at these posts are the brains that tie together the Pentagon's $15 billion network of satellites, radar stations, sensors, and warning systems."[19]

Not without reason, therefore, have the first advances in electronics inevitably had military applications. Electronics have given United States' military power its advantage over potential adversaries for 35 years. "It has supplied," one informed account states, "means for instantaneous communications with any part of the world, the capability for continuous planetwide surveillance and a high degree of precision in weapon guidance. It is difficult, furthermore, to see how we could manage our $125-billion investment in weapons systems or assign and support 2 million uniformed personnel in more than 100 separate locations throughout the world without computer assistance and electronic information storage."[20]

The vital contribution of electronics and computer communications to U.S. military strength is generally recognized. Less attention has been paid to the very active role the military has played in developing new communications technologies. The National Security Agency (NSA), the military unit engaged in a wide variety of unpublicized electronics operations inside and outside the country, has been identified as a hidden "angel" of modern communications research and development.

According to a recent report,

> For many years the agency has been a major source of research
> funds for the computer and telecommunications industries. As a re-
> sult, it has helped shape a series of technological advances that have
> had vast impact on American society . . . . The NSA has also played
> a key role in the development of the modern computer . . . the se-
> cret research funds the agency provided to such companies and insti-
> tutions as the Radio Corporation of America, the International
> Business Machines Corporation and Massachusetts Institute of
> Technology 'hastened the start of the computer age' and fed a stream
> of research and design advances.[21]

As this account indicates, the University too, has played, and continues to play, a major role in research and development carried out
for the system's military arm. In the spring of 1980, *The New York
Times* reported: "Flush with money, and with explicit White House
encouragement, high-ranking Defense Department officials have
been visiting campuses all over the country, offering funds for basic
research in communications, fiber optics, materials, integrated circuits, climatology and even psychology"—in a word, all the areas of
research identified as the leading edges of the information
economy.

The efforts of the war machine have not been rebuffed. Representative of university administration and faculty sentiment is the
reaction of the associate vice president of the University of Texas,
at Austin: "Our people look for grant support wherever they find
it." Cornell, M.I.T., Stanford, and Berkeley "are elbowing one another" to get at these funds.

Now, as in the 1960s, "Nowhere is the complex military-
academic relationship more apparent than at the Massachusetts Institute of Technology. The school gets about $18 million a year in
Pentagon research money, which pays for about 15 percent of cam-
pus research. A large chunk, nearly $3 million, goes to the Re-
search Laboratory for Electronics. The research laboratory is eight
stories of humming computers and flashing lasers. The Pentagon
money helps support 85 professors, 100 researchers and 200 students."[22] Other costly research programs in communications and
electronics, footed by U.S. Navy budgets, study sound and how it
travels through water. This "pure" scientific interest has direct application to anti-submarine and other forms of naval warfare.[23]

Perhaps in gratitude, certainly in self-interest, the business system, and particularly some of the companies mentioned above, reciprocate assistance to the military machine in an equally unpublicized way.

It has long been understood that a significant sector of American industry—aerospace is one striking example—could not survive without military orders. One consequence of decades of heavy arms expenditures is the existence of the "military-industrial complex," a meeting ground of industrial and military interest, personalities, and policies. Yet there is more to the corporate-Armed Forces connection than heavy public expenditures and job opportunities for generals and admirals in the private sector. The recognition by American corporate leadership, *at the highest level*, of its dependence on military power to support its vital worldwide interests and involvements, makes it all the more willing to participate in joint arrangements hardly to be imagined in an open society. One such longstanding "arrangement" has been the connivance of major U.S. companies with military intelligence agencies to monitor private communications.

As early as 1945—the year that simultaneously saw the end of World War II and the launching of the American Century—*Operation Shamrock* was organized. This clandestine activity, with its code name designating good luck, began "when the Army Signals Security Agency approached RCA Global, ITT World Communications and Western Union International, commercial carriers of international telegraphs, for access to their transmissions. The Agency desired to monitor foreign government traffic passing over the facilities of the companies. Understandings were reached with officials as high as the Secretary of Defense, despite advice from the companies' attorneys that the interception would be illegal during peacetime. The arrangements generally gave the Agency access to telegrams of all parties, not just those of foreign governments (the traffic was later used to build files on individuals)."[24] The National Security Agency (NSA) later took over this assignment and continued to monitor the communications flow for more than 20 years.

As computers became the essential elements in international telecommunications, the connection between U.S. Intelligence and the corporate economy was extended. It appears that NSA (the most secret intelligence unit in the country) has had a close collaboration with IBM on the development of computer encryption equipment and, in particular, the creation of the Data Encryption Standard (DES), designed by IBM and certified for use by the National Bureau of Standards. Moreover, the DES is the standard for exported equipment.

What this adds up to is a strong belief that any code developed with DES can be broken by NSA. Given the history of codebreaking and illegal message monitoring of the last few decades, it is not paranoid to imagine that data flows, domestic or transnational, encrypted or not, are vulnerable to U.S. interception and deciphering. In fact, interception of private and governmental international messages has become institutionalized. The *Transnational Data Report* reproduces an item, taken from the *New Statesman*, which indicates that Menwith Hill in the United Kingdom "is alleged to be the biggest telephone-telex interception center in the world. The United States National Security Agency operates this 800-man listening post with the full cooperation of the British Post Office. . . . The facility is said to be the hub of Britain's international communications to, from and within Europe. It is composed of submarine cables and satellite ground stations. This allows interception of all transatlantic traffic, those originating from and directed to Northern and Eastern Europe as well."[25]

Referring to the security of data flowing through modern communication networks, the chairman of the American Federation of Information Processing Societies' (Afips) Panel on Transborder Data Flow carefully notes that "the general problem of providing total security in a multi-user, resource-sharing computer system has not been totally solved—while it may be very difficult, it still may be possible for experts (especially those who have regular access to the system) to capture unauthorized control of the system, and, thereby, obtain access to all data files"[26] If those "experts" work with the original designers of the system, how much more probable is the possibility of unauthorized control?

Further indication, if it were needed, of the high priority the intelligence and military agencies put on cryptography, is that American computer scientists and mathematicians, working in the field

as academics, have been requested, and have acceded, to the unprecedented demand of the National Security Agency to screen
their work prior to its publication.[27]

Ordinarily, the mechanics with which technological domination
over weaker partners is employed are carefully shielded from public scrutiny, both at home and in the dominated nation. Not so in the
United States-Iranian crisis of 1979–1981. *Science* reported that
"as part of a package of sanctions against Iran, former President
Carter on 17 April [1980] proposed an interruption in the Iranians'
use of the ten communication satellites that make up the Intelsat
system . . . A cut-off of this sort would play havoc with Iran's
funds transfers, with its airline scheduling, and with its telephone
and television service. In all, 70 percent of Iran's international
telecommunication needs are served by the satellites of
Intelsat."[28] It was also revealed that the President conferred with
the head of the Comsat corporation, who serves as manager of the
Intelsat system, about this proposal.

In this instance, the United States initiative to penalize Iran by
disrupting its international communications was unable to be realized for a variety of technical and political reasons. But the intent
and will to do so were unmistakeably present.

Later in the same crisis, when the U.S. military project to pluck
the American hostages from its embassy in Teheran was undertaken, the question arose of how the sizable number of planes and
helicopters escaped the detection of the Iranian air warning system. Iranian President Bani-Sadr had this explanation:

> We have said so many times that the Americans had made our coun-
> try dependent on them through many ways . . . . They have given
> us our radar systems, and they have installed it themselves, so they
> know where to pass and not be seen on our radar. We have to put an
> independent system on our borders to prevent this kind of action.[29]

In sum, the national sovereignty of a nation dependent on someone else's control of space communications is uncertain at best, as
the Iranian experience demonstrates. One additional account rein-
forces this conclusion:

> At an informal colloqium held at UCLA [University of California,
> Los Angeles] this spring [1978], a representative of Hughes Aircraft
> Company, to questioning by the audience, admitted that Indonesia's

'Palapa' satellite—designed by Hughes and orbited by NASA—could be 'turned off' on command from Hughes or the U.S. Department of Defense.

The report's author concluded that as Indonesia comes to rely more and more on its satellite-communications system, it will become more and more susceptible to coercion exercised by those who control, most decisively, its national communications.[30]

NATIONAL SOVEREIGNTY AND THE NEW COMMUNICATIONS TECHNOLOGIES

Underlying the applications of the new communications technologies—transnational border data flow, remote sensing (discussed in the next chapter), and direct satellite broadcasting—are commonalities. First, there is utilization of the most advanced communication technology: satellites, photographic and electronic scanning instrumentation, sophisticated transmission networks, data processing systems, and advanced computer communications. Second, in each of these new technologies there exists an American technical advantage, derived mainly from the enormous research and development expenditures of the American military machine over the last 30 years. (It has been noted that some of these expenditures have been covertly channeled through some of the largest U.S. transnational corporations.) Third, each of these new communications technologies and its application produces a wide range of benefits that are unequally distributed and differentially enjoyed. The unequal distribution of power and wealth inside and between countries makes it inevitable, unless there is a determined effort to overcome it, that the new technologies will further accentuate existing inequalities and discriminations.

Satellite communications and remote sensing are accessible mostly to those with the means to pay for the relatively high costs of operation. Almost automatically, huge, private companies and a few powerful governments are the chief beneficiaries—though superficially, the instrumentation appears to be open for use to all. Transnational border data flows, too, are mostly comprised of the messages sent by the transnational companies within their own corporate systems to their branch plants and subsidiaries around the world. Individual and nonprofit access to such facilities immediately confront the hurdle of payment.

Finally, there is a fourth commonality in these advanced communications technologies and their applications, which together with the preceding ones helps to explain the growing international questioning of the United States' favorite doctrine of the free flow of information. Alongside the technical advantage enjoyed by, and the benefits accruing to already powerful, mostly U.S. institutions and organizations from their ability to utilize the new technologies, there is the overriding matter of national sovereignty. Each of these new and related technologies has the capability to disregard national boundaries and national decision making. Direct broadcasting from a satellite passes over a country's broadcasting system. Electronic transnational border data flows move silently and effortlessly across frontiers without interuption or scrutiny.

In sum, a combination of modern communication technologies have been developed, installed, and are operating, which ignore and bypass national decision making. They are not however, at the disposition of some benign international authority, intent on the reduction of longstanding gaps in living standards between the privileged few and the disadvantaged many. On the contrary, these advanced forms of communication are available now, for the most part, to already-dominant United States governmental and private economic interests and instrumentalities.

At the same time as these technologies reinforce the TNCs and assist the integration of capitalist enterprise worldwide, they also serve to weaken the authority of the national state, which is unable to cope with the tremendous economic and technological power of these transnational structures formalistically operating under their domain.*

The most recent communications advance, remote sensing (the subject of the next chapter) compounds further the difficulties of the national state in exercising autonomous decision making in matters vital to its independence and the well-being of its people.

*In a recent study which describes and reveals secret American communication installations in Australia, the author inscribes his book, "For A Sovereign Australia." Desmond Ball, *A suitable piece of real estate*, Sydney, Australia: Hale & Iremonger, 1980.

Notes to Chapter Five

1. William L. Fishman, "International data flow: Personal privacy and other matters," February 3, 1978. Fishman was Assistant Director for International Communications, Office of Telecommunications Policy, Executive Office of the President. Fishman now holds a different post in the Government.

2. "multinational corporate activity . . . is expected to account for 16–20% of the world's output by 1985." William L. Fishman, *op. cit.*

3. Arthur L. Robinson, "Microelectronics: Defense Department looks to the 1980's,"*Science*, September 22, 1978, *201* pp. 1112–1113.

4. Richard Burt, "Experts believe laser weapons could transform warfare in 80's," *The New York Times*, February 10, 1980, p. 1. Also, *The New York Times*, December 10, 1978, editorial.

5. *Bulletin of the American Society for Information Science*, August 1978, *4* (6), p. 12.
    The vice president for International and corporate Operations of *Tymshare, Inc.*, comments: "It is rather awesome to reflect on how little is known and understood about information movement and its economic/social value. This applies both to transborder (international) and to intraborder (national) flows." Alden Heintz, "The computer services industry," in *Data regulation: European and Third World realities.*Uxbridge, England: Online, 1978.

6. Jake Kirchner, "Impact report sparks ire of delegates to TDF '79,"*Computerworld*, December 17, 1979, p. 17.

7. *Datamation*, March 1978, p. 203.

8. Bernard Ostry, "Industry should regulate data flow," *Transnational Data Report*, October 1980, *3* (6) p. 10.

9. *Datamation*, March 1978, p. 201.

10. Robert B. White, before the Subcommittee on International Operations, Foreign Relations Committee, U.S. Senate, June 10, 1977. Also, *Computerworld*, January 22, 1979.

11. Alexander I. Nacamuli, "SWIFT: Objectives, Standardization, availability, auditability, security, privacy and liability," *Transnational Data Report*, October 1980, *3* (6) p. 7.

12. *International Herald Tribune*, September 4, 1978.

13. Judith A. Werdel & Richard A. Steele, "The information age: Worldwide data warfare?", *Bulletin of the American Society for Information Science*, August 1978, *4* (6), p. 12.

14. Robert A. Bennett, "Currency deals shown to surge at U.S. banks," *The New York Times*, June 23, 1980, p.D1.

15.   "Stateless money," *Business Week*, August 21, 1978, pp. 76–94, emphasis added.

16.   Will sparks, "The flow of information and the new technology of money," paper presented to the Conference on World Communications: Decisions for the Eighties, Annenberg School of Communications, Philadelphia, Pa., May 12–14, 1980.

17.   Report of the Group of Experts on International Standards of Accounting and Reporting, E/C/10/33, United Nations, New York, October 18, 1977. Also, Frederick Andrews, "Unifying rules in accounting," *The New York Times*, June 4, 1980, p. D2.

18.   The case of the former president of Lockheed Corporation, Carl Kotchian "could shed new light on the government's sensitive, often tangled relationships with major U.S. corporations overseas. In particular, it could document the way some American companies have provided cover for U.S. intelligence agents abroad." David Ignatius, "Foreign bribery trials may show U.S. knew of some payments."*The Wall Street Journal*, October 5, 1978.

19.   William J. Broad, "Computers and the U.S. Military don't mix," *Science*, March 14, 1980, *207*, pp. 1183–1187.

20.   G. P. Dinneen & H. C. Frick "Electronics and national defense: A case study," *Science*, March 18, 1977, *195* pp. 1151–1155.

21.   David Burnham "Security agency plays major role in policies on communications," *The New York Times*, February 1, 1979, p. 1.

22.   Robert Reinhold, "Pentagon renews ties with colleges," *The New York Times*, May 13, 1980, p.C 1.

23.   Drew Middleton, "Expert predicts a big U.S. gain in sub warfare," *The New York Times*, February 18, 1979.

24.   Greg Lipscomb, "Private and public defenses against Soviet interception of U.S. telecommunications: Problems and policy points," April 1978, Working paper W-78-6, Program on Information Resources Policy, Harvard University, Cambridge, Mass., p. 15.

25.   "U. K. journal reveals joint UK-US listening post," *Transnational Data Report*, October 1980, *3* (6), p.12.

26.   Dr. Rein Turn, "Observations on transborder data flows," *AFIPS*, May 1978, mimeo, p. 4.

27.   Richard Severo, "Researchers to permit pre-publication review by U.S.," *The New York Times*, November 1, 1980, p. 14.

28.   William J. Broad, "No go for satellite sanctions against Iran," *Science*, May 16, 1980, *208*, pp.685–686.

29.   *The New York Times*, April 27, 1980, p. 1.

30.   Robert E. Jacobson, "Satellite business systems and the concept of the dispersed enterprise: An end to national sovereignty?", paper presented to the East-West Communications Institute Summer Seminar on Transnational Communications Enterprises and National Policies, Honolulu, Hawaii, August 6–9, 1978.

chapter six

Planetary Resource Information Flows: A New Dimension of Hegemonic Power or Global Social Utility?

Indeed, the threat to independence in the late twentieth century from the new electronics could be greater than was colonialism itself.

Anthony Smith, The geopolitics of information. New York: Oxford, 1980, p. 176.

Computer communications, based in a few, advanced industrial countries, are facilitating the integration of peripheral regions and territories into the world business system. At the same time as this integration proceeds, most national states find their power and authority diminishing. Electronic communications enable transnational corporate managers routinely to circumvent and increasingly to disregard any state's authority on matters of great national interest. Yet the nation state is the only political entity capable of restraining super-corporations from running the world to suit themselves.

With the advent of communication satellites, the territorial space of the nation—its total environmental security—becomes problematic. The satellite can be directed to perform a remarkably detailed scrutiny of terrestial and oceanic phenomena. Termed *remote sensing*, it is defined by a United Nations report "as a system of methods for identifying the nature and/or determining the condition of objects on the earth's surface and of phenomena on, below, or above it, by means of observation from airborne or spaceborne platforms."[1]

Remote sensing is a very recent development, only a few years old. The first experimental remote sensing satellite, *Landsat* 1, was launched by the National Aeronautics and Space Administration (NASA) in 1972. An environmental, as distinct from an earth-scanning, remote sensing satellite, for weather observation and prediction, began operating in 1966, under the jurisdiction of the National Oceanic and Atmospheric Administration in the Department of Commerce. A Data Center (EROS), which disseminates some of the data derived from the sensing satellites, began operating in 1974. A second *Landsat* was launched in 1975 and a third in 1978. Only *Landsat* 3 is currently working.

The uses to which remote sensing data have already been applied are numerous and impressive. These include crop monitoring, mineral and fuels exploration, forest management, national resource inventories, flood control, pinpointing fish concentrations for the fishing industry, identifying frost edge for the citrus industry, and charting the Gulf Stream currents. Some specific applications are described by one oil company. The data were used "for locating prime uranium targets, laying out pipeline routes through mountains, extrapolating geologic models to upgrade offshore drilling locations, pinpointing hot spots of concern in our refineries, mapping ancient burnout zones in coal fields, predicting areas of intensely fractured rocks for safety control in coal mining . . . and, of course, preliminary oil and gas exploration."[2]

As the field is still in its infancy, it is certain that its uses will multiply. Already it is clear that the potential of remote sensing for providing physical information about all areas of the globe, for human benefit, is phenomenal.

REMOTE SENSING: THE QUINTESSENTIAL INTERNATIONAL ACTIVITY

As an enumeration of existing applications demonstrates, the technique of remote sensing suggests one central assumption—that it will serve the general public wherever it is carried out. Yet this crucial expectation cannot be taken for granted.

Remote sensing, utilizing orbiting space satellites, is an *international* activity. Spatially, territorially, nothing less than the earth itself is the compass of the sensing process. Consequently, unless remote sensing is treated as a global public service function, fully in accord with the needs, wishes, and aspirations of the populations and regions the satellite passes over and surveys, the process can create suspicion and discord, rather than support and appreciation.

For this reason, the *social* use of remote sensing must be assured if it is to be acceptable to the world community, whose space and geography it routinely intrudes upon. It is precisely because this assurance is not yet forthcoming that remote sensing has become a source of unease and disagreement. The reasons for this disappointing direction of the development of a new technology are to be found in the structure of the economy in which the process originated.

REMOTE SENSING AS A SOURCE OF SYSTEMIC HEGEMONY

Though remote sensing is the quintessential international activity, its utilization for national and private advantage has been sought from the outset. The power groups which occupy commanding positions in the United States have been awake, from the beginning, to the opportunities offered them by remote sensing. To capitalize on these possibilities, the government—on the behalf of specific clusters of corporate power and the military machine—has been the prime mover in the development and installation of the new communication and information technology. Remote sensing and other high technology capabilities, are considered strategic factors in the maintenance of the American global business empire. Admission by U.S. officials of these intentions is not difficult to document. For example, former President Carter's Science Advisor and Director of the Office of Science and Technology, Dr. Frank Press, assured a Congressional commmittee in 1979, that "so far as the Europeans are concerned, they're starting in a position so far behind us that all their activity right now is an effort just to get going. The resources that we commit to remote sensing and other applications in space far exceeds all that they do together."

This being so, the legislators could rely on the fact that the Science Advisor "can't conceive that this Administration or succeeding ones would allow remote sensing technology of other countries to supersede our own and become technologically more advanced. As you know, the President's commitment to maintaining leadership includes and subsumes remote sensing as one of the many areas in space where we want to maintain our leadership."[3]

Supporting this view of "leadership," the executive vice president of the Comsat Corporation, a company totally involved with space communications, informed the legislators: "While it's unrealistic for us to assume that we can maintain a U.S. monopoly on Earth sensing, I think we should at least aspire to maintain a leadership role."[4]

And still another voice from the corporate sector observed, in more practical terms: "The United States cannot afford to lose the remaining advantages that have come from developing technologies that have allowed us to become primary finders and developers of the world's non-renewable resources."[5]

Becoming "the primary finders and developers of the world's non-renewable resources" is no small achievement when the limits of the earth's bountifulness are increasingly apparent and the struggle for access to scarce resources intensifies. "Leadership" in space, and in remote sensing in particular, contributes to this end. It does this by wresting information about areas from those who have a first claim on such knowledge—the inhabitants of the area.

Consider the perspective on this issue of a high ranking official in the Department of State's International Environmental and Scientific Affairs Bureau:

> One [problem] concerns the question of sovereignty over information pertaining to natural resources. We find that many developing countries guard their natural resources quite jealously and are considerably concerned that advanced countries might be able to exploit them to their disadvantage. That has motivated a number of countries to assert sovereign control and sovereign claims over information and data concerning their natural resources that is in the hands of others. *This is a claim that, of course, we can't agree with and it is a claim put forth strongly by a number of developing countries . . . we do not consider the question of sovereignty negotiable. That is the question of sovereignty over information in the hands of others.*[6]

Under this interpretation, "leadership" in remote sensing technology permits the "leader" to assume rights over the information obtained by remote sensing, while at the same time denying the nation whose territories have been surveyed the right to claim sovereignty over its natural resource information. This is a neat construal of international law. With this justification in hand, the United States already "has developed large data bases on the resources of developing nations based on information gathered in remote sensing satellites."[7] Thus, the results deriving from unilateral capability permit the U.S. to secure a comprehensive inventory of the physical features of any nation, regardless of that state's willingness to have such a geographical profile developed. And, further, it allows the U.S. to process the data secured, for whichever purposes it may desire.

Less legalistically inclined, Senator Adlai Stevenson, chairman of the Senate subcommittee designated to consider remote sensing legislation, stressed *force majeur* in determining that *"We* have strategic interests in the world's resources."[8] What could be permitted to stand in the way of *our* strategic interests? To make sure that, in fact, nothing can stand in the way, the military establishment enters the picture.

Actually, remote sensing, *from its inception*, has been a military project, affording the armed forces of the imperial system a critical advantage in global deployment of force and in gathering the intelligence necessary for intervention and military maneuver. This was nicely put by Comsat's executive vice president:

> Specifically, the reason for carrying out Defense Department collection [of data] activities is to be prepared for some kind of a military contingency, or to know more about what adversaries are doing. Typically, the uses for data on the civil side are not in the same parts of the world.[9]

In fact, the data collecting capability of the U.S. military is so highly developed that it creates a problem of intelligence merely to mention it. For example, Senator Stevenson, the chairman of the Senate subcommittee on Science, Technology, and Space, complains that remote sensing "is a difficult area to discuss because everything is classified, and *most of those on the civil side don't know what it is we're talking about. But there are some who do."*[10]

Who are these "some who do?"

Those who do know what the issues of remote sensing are about are mostly, though not necessarily, in the private, corporate sector, working for or managing those companies with a material stake in the earth's resources. These include firms engaged in resource exploration and exploitation, manufacturers of communications hardware, and data processors who take the raw information secured by the sensing satellite and refine it into usable, custom-specified packages.

In these companies there is no lack of expertise. For example, there is the 'instructional' role of the *Geosat Committee, Inc.*, an organization "sponsored by 100 U.S. and non-U.S. international oil, gas, mineral and engineering-geological companies who produce more than half of the nation's non-renewable energy and mineral resources."[11] This committee 'coaches' the National Aeronautics and Space Administration (NASA), the U.S. Geological Survey, and other governmental agencies on the technical issues of interest to its members. [12] NASA's Administrator is pleased to inform Congress that "we are continuing to work with the *Geosat Committee* to explore ways to satisfy the needs of the petroleum and mining industries."[13]

An indication of how these needs are "satisfied" may be appreciated with a glimpse at practices in another natural resource exploratory high technology. According to a report in *Science*, "Consortia of oil companies have entered into agreements with the federal government to drill test wells for the sole purpose of gathering geologic data, *but those data are not made public until the participating companies have bid on leases to drill for oil and gas nearby.*"[14]

How much more effective remote sensing data may be, in providing these same companies with privileged information on resource locations *globally*, can well be imagined. Not to be taken into account are the interests of nations and peoples as their resources are snatched up by private combinations able to take advantage of their special access to natural resource data.

There is also the expertise and interest of the 'value added' information firms that process the raw data and that combine and integrate the data, secured by satellite, with other information sources stored in commercial data banks. *Lockheed Electronics*, a subsidiary of the Lockheed Corporation, is a leader in this field. And *Information World* reports that "a lively business has sprung up in processing and enhancing Landsat imagery. Bendix Aerospace Systems and General Electric both use computers to process and improve imagery for specific purposes . . . TRW, IBM and the Earth Satellite Corporation have done extensive work on improving Landsat's product."*

The third element in the private corporate sector involved with remote sensing comprises the electronics hardware manufacturers and the communication corporations who carry on the business of information transmission. As is evident in the preceding paragraph, sometimes these companies are information processors in their own right.

Among these three corporate groupings—mining and mineral, data processing, and hardware and communication—there is expertise to spare but their interests do not necessarilty coincide and sometimes they conflict. One unifying factor, however, is an overall agreement on the necessity and desirability of eventually utilizing the new scientific-technological capability of remote sensing for profit making and political intelligence under the management of American corporate business.

PRIVATE ASSUMPTION OF
A PUBLICLY SUPPORTED TECHNOLOGY

Since the second world war, a number of new technologies derived from huge investments of public funds, and which carry the promise of great public benefit, have been diverted to profit making and hegemonic ends. This practice is especially observable in the domain of communications. Remote sensing technology now seems slated for a similar fate.

The expenditures that financed the development and creation of this remarkable technological phenomenon were made by the federal government. An exact account is unavailable because much of the costs are inseparable from other communication-space activities. Taking this into account, one authoritative analyst stated that "if one goes back over the past 15 or 20 years to determine how

Information World, May 1980, *2* (4), p. 12–20.

much the U.S. Government has spent in these areas, it is very difficult to run down that number, but it exceeds billions of dollars."[15]

By the end of the 1970s, remote sensing was an operational technology and Congress took up the matter of what should be done
with this important activity, which still resided in the governmental sector. The discussions are instructive for they reveal quite
straightforwardly the politico-economic mechanisms with which
late 20th century American capitalism operates. Most striking of
all, and perhaps to be expected, is the paramount role of the government in developing, maintaining, and assuring the profit-
making interests of the corporate sector in new areas of the
economy.

In early 1979, two bills were introduced in Congress "to establish
an institutional framework for an operational remote-sensing system to gather data by satellite on the Earth's resources and environment."[16] One bill, sponsored by Senator Adlai Stevenson,
recommended that a government entity, NASA, have the initial
operational responsibility which eventually would be transferred to
the private sector. The other bill, sponsored by Senator Harrison
Schmitt, proposed that a private entity *immediately* take over the
operational service, with no intermediary period of governmental
management.

Both the bills and their sponsors were agreed that private management of the system was desirable and necessary. Only the timing of the private takeover separated the two proposals. However,
the reasons for deferring private operation of the system provide
unusual illumination of present-day governmental-corporate relationships.

In November 1979, President Carter announced the designation
of the Department of Commerce's National Oceanic and Atmospheric Administration (NOAA) as the agency "to manage all
operational civilian remote sensing activities from space." At the
same time, the President, following the recommendations of Senators Stevenson and Schmitt, insisted also that "The Commerce Department will seek ways to further private sector opportunities in
civilian remote sensing activities, through joint ventures with industry, a quasi-government corporation, leasing, etc., *with the goal
of eventual operation of these activities by the private sector*."[17]

For the time being, therefore, and for an uncertain number of
years to come, remote sensing remains a governmental function.

However, the intention to turn the activity over to the private sector has been announced unequivocally. The National Oceanic and Atmospheric Administration's administrator, Richard A. Frank, in 1980 confirmed the presidentially announced intention. "The private sector will eventually own and operate the Landsat System."*

What may be expected to occur in this transitional period has been set down unambiguously in the records of the Senate subcommittee chaired by Senator Stevenson. Here the business community has expressed its views—it would be more appropriate to say "announced its terms"—for undertaking the remote sensing enterprise in the future. What these 'terms' stipulate are likely, but not inevitably, to provide a guide for developments in this field in the years ahead. Though room remains for public initiatives and social pressure, the course has been outlined and measures announced that will permit corporate control of the new technology *when the time is deemed appropriate.*

PROPOSED FEATURES OF A FUTURE, FOR-PROFIT REMOTE SENSING ENTITY

(1)The Disposition of Past Public Investment

The first issue to be faced in the transferring of operational responsibility for remote sensing from a governmental to a private entity is how to handle the existing plants and equipment, all of which have been financed out of public funds. The recommendation of the business community, taking innumerable precedents into account, is direct and forthright: Give it away free of charge to the private entity assuming the remote sensing function. One businessman put it this way: "Whatever plant and equipment and other related investments have been made that are determined by the new organization to be useful for its purposes should be looked upon as a contribution by the Government to start off this operation."[18]

(2) Research and Development

Once the existing plant and equipment have been donated by the government to the private entity, the next question relates to the

*Business Week, June 30, 1980, p. 49.

heavy costs of research and development, which probably have to be increased if American capitalism is to retain its world 'leadership' in this strategically important sector. And there is no lack of awareness of this necessity. On the first page of an interagency governmental report on civil space remote sensing, issued in 1979, for example, it was noted that "U.S. leadership will be increasingly challenged by foreign competition in all areas of civil remote sensing."[19]

Who should undertake these expenditures? Again, the business community is unambiguous about its expectations. In the same interagency report, it was found that the opinions of the private sector are "universally agreed that the government should continue to conduct research and development programs in remote sensing systems and applications even after private operations are established."[20]

NASA's former administrator, Dr. Robert A. Frosch, agreed that the governmental role in R & D for remote sensing would have to remain substantial well after a private, for-profit, operating entity was established: "I think there would have to be a continuing governmental role in R & D, partly because we need that continuing stimulus for progress which would not certainly in the initial provision of services be easily accommodated while an outside entity was building up a market."[21]

(3) Providing a Market for Remote Sensing Data

The main activity of a private business established to operate the remote sensing function would be to sell the data secured from the sensing process. Who would buy that data? Indeed, who buys what is now being produced? In 1978, the Landsat data market showed the following user breakdown:[22]

The largest user by far of remote sensing data is the federal government. The business community, as well as other informed par-

Sector	Dollar Value of Market	% of Market
Federal government	$2,550,876	52
Private industry	579,950	12
Foreign	1,340,539	27
Other: e.g., universities & state & local governments	374,770	9

ties, expect this pattern of use to continue. Business views here, too, are unanimous and forthright: "Perhaps the most important private sector conviction is that the federal government is now and will continue to make up the largest share of the market for such sensing data and services. Indeed, one company felt the government must provide 75% of the market share to make private investment attractive."[23] This was also the opinion of NASA's administrator: "In fact, one of the key questions in establishing any private entity as the favored or chosen instrument . . . is the question of the establishment of the Government as, in effect, a single buyer from that single source, because I think that's likely to be the initial economic guarantee that makes such an enterprise a viable one as it gets started, and as it faces the problem of aggregating and developing for the non-Government market."[24]

The rich-blooded risk-avoidance that the private sector exhibits in its approach to remote sensing is nicely summarized by the executive vice president of the Comsat corporation:

The Government would have to commit itself to buy its needs from such a system and not to do them by a parallel program. The Government would have to agree not to compete, and the Government would have to agree to buy from us a minimum amount, so many dollars per year, for example, so we'd have some assurance of that type of revenue.[25]

The vice president of the *General Electric Corporation* chimed in:

Remember: Everybody recognizes the fact that the private offering initially has to serve principally the large Government market. Nobody, Comsat or anybody else, is stepping up without recognition that the Government must get its act together, and essentially agree to purchase enough to make the initial entry viable.[26]

Recapitulating, the "required government actions" the corporate sector insists the Government accede to before private enterprise assumes the remote sensing function include: giving away the existing facilities free of charge, governmental obligation to undertake future R & D expenditure, governmental assurance not to enter into any competition as well as to guarantee a fixed market for remote sensing data, and government management of the international negotiations which global remote sensing activities necessitate.

This less-than-timid set of demands may be understood as the checklist submitted by the corporate sector to govern future decision making on remote sensing. The extent to which this agenda will be followed will be affected by many presently unforeseen factors. However, it will be determined ultimately by the level of opposition, if any, in what is now an uninformed and therefore indifferent public opinion.

Still, the public aspects of the remote sensing function are so overriding that uncontested adoption of the corporate agenda cannot be considered a foregone conclusion. For in truth, the terms that the corporate sector imposes as preconditions for its direct assumption of remote sensing are the strongest arguments for maintaining public control of the new technology. All the vital elements in the operation require the public's financial support and governmental guarantees.

To be sure, governmental oversight and operation of remote sensing, *of the sort now occurring,* cannot be viewed as protective of the public's interest. The present governmental role in remote sensing, as with many other important functions in the economy, serves a corporate, not a popular, constituency. Yet it is the public that underwrites the entire effort.

Another unsettling element in the corporate scenario for remote sensing is that the high profits and insurance against losses that the agenda stipulates are only the *visible* costs of private enterprise in what is essentially a public undertaking. Less calculable but more longlasting costs are the likely consequences of the privatization of remote sensing. These concern a deepening information inequality in the society at large.

INFORMATION INEQUALITY AS
AN OUTGROWTH OF MARKET FORCES

Actually, the management of remote sensing involves nothing less than the paramount issue of how technology is to be utilized. Or, otherwise put, what or who will constitute the institutional determinants of the new technology? It is these determinants which directly affect the *kind* of information that will be produced and disseminated. This is so because the kind of information that is sought, organized, and made available depends ultimately on who the primary user will be. The primary user, in turn, is a function of how decisions are organized institutionally.

To wit, once remote sensing—or any other information technology, for that matter—is the instrument of a private, profit-making entity, market factors determine who the primary user will be. And market criteria insist, inflexibly, that the user must be identified on an ability-to-pay principle. Insofar as remote sensing information gathering is concerned, the ability-to-pay yardstick confers decision-making authority on the treasuries of the mining and information hardware companies, or on the Government, acting as surrogate for those interests. Social well-being receives no ballots in this kind of voting.

Local governmental and public interest groups are fully aware of this dynamic, which largely excludes their participation. The national Conference on State Legislatures, for instance, informed Congress that "the needs of public-sector users would not necessarily be adequately met in an environment where profit and loss are the major considerations." The National Governors Association elaborated on this viewpoint:

> Due to the public service nature of remote sensing, it is recommended that the system be Federally owned and operated for at least near term. The states' major concern, particularly in regards to the ground segment is that a privately operated system could tend to develop standardized products in response to the needs of large, aggregated markets and reduce or eliminate marginal products for limited markets in an attempt to increase profitability. Although this approach would provide very efficient and responsible service to the large markets, it may reduce the amount of very useful service to a wide range of users, such as State and local governments.[27]

Demand, expressed through the price system in a profit-making context, inevitably works to the advantage of the strongest forces in the market. When the product is information, this means that the strongest buyer, in addition to having priority access to the information product, largely determines as well the *kind* of information product that is made available. What is demanded—if it is secured by ability to pay—is produced.

MARKET DETERMINATION OF TECHNOLOGY TRANSFER

Information demand, determined on an ability-to-pay basis (the essential market desideratum), results in a very specific kind of information, a type which is of special value to those who can afford to pay for it. There is yet another aspect of market-determined information demand which further exacerbates inequalities in the social sphere. This has to do with what is called technology transfer.

In brief, technology transfer refers, along with the actual hardware, to the entire range of expertise required to manage and utilize knowledgably any technology and its related processes. In the information realm, and with remote sensing in particular, technology transfer is especially important, because if it does not occur in a meaningful way the recipient of the information, however benefitted by the data, *remains dependent on the information provider and the technology supplier.*

The more developed technology becomes and the less adequately it is transferred, the more likely the extension of dependency. Actually, this is one of the central but concealed assumptions in the 'leadership' rhetoric, continuously expressed by United States'policy makers. Leadership in technology is a euphemism for the maintenance of domination in the technical sphere and all the cultural and economic areas that connect to it.

For example, early in 1980 Harold Brown, the Secretary of Defense, announced "that the United States was prepared to sell China a ground station for receiving information from the Landsat Earth Resources Satellite, which has military applications." In the same breath, this politically charged development was minimized by other U.S. officials, because, they said, "the United States controls what information will be fed to the Chinese ground station."[28]

Similar situations and relationships prevail inside as well as outside countries. Thus, some of the less influential sectors in the domestic economy, the states and municipalities, voice the fear that they may be denied adequate technology transfer if the remote sensing function is delivered over to private control.

It is recognized that "basic organizational imperatives of industry and state and local government result in the private sector (as an entrepreneur) being unsuited to provide technology transfer. After all, it is not in the interest of private firms to truly transfer technology since such an action would eliminate subsequent opportunities for business."[29]

In sum, a privately operated remote sensing system is a source of inadequate technology transfer and also, therefore, a guarantor of greater information dependency. The implications are the same for the impact of such a system, whether it is domestically or internationally operative. Seen from this perspective, unless strong counter measures are introduced internationally and nationally to insure that remote sensing's potential is fully comprehended by a *general usership* the new technology is almost certain to be an agent for increased information inequality.

FUTURE DEVELOPMENTS

For the time being, responsibility for remote sensing has been placed in the hands of a government entity, the National Oceanic and Atmospheric Administration. The temporary assignment of responsibility for remote sensing to a governmental entity is largely because no private company has expressed an interest in taking over the operation *at this time*, due to uncertainty of markets and profitability. But all firms "wish the door kept open."[30]

It is felt that "long bargaining will have to take place before a final deal is struck." *Business Week** adds that "at least half a dozen aerospace and communications companies are considering making bids." These include some *Fortune 500* familiar standbys: Comsat General, General Electric, Hughes Aircraft, Western Union, Lockheed Missiles and Space, TRW, and International Business Machines.

How remote sensing will be administered in the years ahead, therefore, remains an open issue. The special opportunities that this new technology offers to hegemonic power, along with the monopoly privileges it confers on those with access to its processed data flows, suggest strongly that control of remote sensing will not be yielded easily by those that presently enjoy its benefits—the military and the Government, as trustee for the corporate sector.

Whether unilateral U.S. control can be maintained in the face of an almost universal insistence on an international regimen for the

*Business Week, June 30, 1980, p.49.

increasing technical capability to map and inventory the world's physical features is at best uncertain. The technical monopoly on space satellites is surely a waning asset. But the maintenance of control over the analysis of the raw data secured in the sensing process is another matter entirely. Though it, too, depends on the technical capacity of the analyser, this ability is likely to remain an area of long term American superiority, for it is reliant on computer communications mastery, a field of continued American strength. As one account puts it "the collection of data is only half the story—and perhaps not the more difficult or the more important half. The treatment of the data, and its transformation into intelligible and useful information, poses an even larger series of problems."[31]

Remote sensing therefore poses two issues, both strongly affecting the independence of nations. First, there is the elementary inviolability of national space. There can be little doubt that remote sensing is indifferent to this historical national prerogative. Then, there is the differential capacity to utilize the data derived from such activity. As one report carefully notes, "there is little doubt that sophisticated institutions can use remote-sensing data to increase their political and economic power relative to less sophisticated institutions. Knowledge of likely oil deposits, projections of crop yields and better estimates of mineral concentration can help developed world governments and multinational corporations make better political judgements and better bids in international markets."[32]

Stated more bluntly, the ability to use the information relayed by satellite photographing and other processes currently employed is largely in the hands of TNCs and their powerful allies in the governmental and intelligence bureaucracies. Why, for instance, should the knowledge of crop yields outside their own boundaries be of value to "developed governments"? One difficult-to-avoid explanation is that such information will permit political exactions to be imposed when such information suggests agricultural failures and food dependencies.

In 1974, for instance, a program got underway to forecast global crops. Called Large Area Crop Inventory Experiment (LACIE), it combined the efforts of NASA, USDA (U.S. Department of Agriculture), and NOAA. Hardly a random selection, attention was concentrated first on estimating the Soviet wheat crop in 1977 and 1978.[33]

It cannot be overlooked that, at the present time, this capability is an American monopoly. "Most of the analytical expertise, as well as the Landsat technology, is American." The primary (raw) data is available to all comers. The processed data is handled quite differently. This material "is considered proprietary information." There is a big gap dividing most countries from the United States on the disposition of analysed information.

> Most [UN] delegations feel that the dissemination of primary data as well as analysed information to third parties should not be to the detriment, economic or otherwise, of the sensed nation. In opposition to this, the United States maintains that analysed information is the work product of, and the property of, the analyser and therefore should not be treated in the same manner as primary data.[34]

In short, United States computer communications capability, governmentally and privately organized, serves well the hegemonic strivings of the TNCs. A review of the entire process makes this abundantly clear:

> An immense information advantage enjoyed by the United States comes from its ownership of a vast earth resources intelligence system composed by scanning satellites, communication facilities, large computer processing facilities, and the associated scientific knowhow to design and manage the system and to analyse the results. The ERTS and LANDSAT satellites produce vital information about crop conditions, the stocks and movement of fish, the growth and health of forests, and geological formations and deposits. These data are organized in a useful way by various agencies of the U.S. government and can be used to formulate American trade and investment policies.
>
> The U.S. government and, to a lesser extent, U.S. corporations, thus are armed with foreknowledge regarding market conditions, and take advantage of their knowledge. The nations that do not have the analytical capabilities to reduce the data to useful knowledge, thus feel that they are giving away a precious resource (strategic economic information) without receiving much in return.[35]

It is not only that the less technologically advanced nations are "not receiving much in return." The information about their own natural resources may be used directly against their interests by TNCs, intelligence services, and ill disposed governments.

In sum, remote sensing, a scientific achievement with a tremendous potential for contributing to global well-being, began as a means and continues to serve the interests of American state power and corporate industry—though some lesser benefits have accrued to other nations and groups as well. Additionally, remote sensing as presently practiced usurps national sovereignty over natural resources and permits such information to be extracted and transmitted by an external power over which the sensed nation has no authority whatsoever.[36]

Despite what appears to be a position of American invincibility, remote sensing's dependence on international agreement for its complete utilization introduces a considerable and growing check on arbitrary usage and monopolistic advantage. United Nations' bodies continue to review a broad set of issues—economic, legal, cultural, and technical—that are outgrowths of this new technology. Sentiment in international forums is heavily in favor of *international decision making* which removes the scanning capability from national, essentially United States, domination.[37]

Domestically too, the public interest cannot fail to be expressed more strongly as recognition grows of the potential utilization of remote sensing for social purposes, while observing its present custodianship and application largely on behalf of private benefit and hegemonic power.

It seems, therefore, that the struggle for access to and the demand for equality of information derived from remote sensing will continue to be expressed and pressure will increase for a genuine social utilization and application of this information. This struggle will be part of a larger effort that will seek to curb transnational corporate power in all spheres of the international economy. Some of the dimensions of this overarching effort are considered in the final two chapters.

Notes to Chapter Six

1.   Report of the United Nations Panel Meeting on the Establishment and Implementation of Research: Programmes in Remote Sensing, UN Doc. A/AC/105/98, January 20, 1972, Par. 3.

2. Hearings before the subcommittee on Science, Technology and Space of the Committee on Commerce, Science and Transportation, United States Senate, 96th Congress, First Session, on S. 663 and S. 875, Part 2, July 31st, 1979, U. S. G.P.O., Washington, D. C., 1979, p. 287. Afterwards referred to as *Hearings*.

3. *Hearings, op. cit.*, Part 1, April 9 & 11, 1979, pp. 50–51.

4. *Ibid.*, testimony of Dr. John McLucas, p. 179.

5. *Ibid.*, testimony of Frederick B. Henderson, President of the *Geosat Committee*, p. 204.

6. *Ibid.*, testimony of Dr. Irwin Pikus, p.172, emphasis added.

7. Rex Malik & E. Drake Lundell, Jr., "Global net may serve Third World," *Computer World*, June 26, 1978.

8. *Hearings*, Senator Adlai Stevenson, p. 209, emphasis added.

9. *Ibid.*, pp. 209–209.

10. *Ibid.*, emphasis added.

11. *Ibid.*, p.199.

12. *Ibid.*, p.45.

13. *Ibid.*, p. 62.

14. Richard A. Kerr "Explorer: Can oil and science mix?", *Science*, February 8, 1980 *207* p.627, emphasis added.

15. *Hearings*, Part 2, *op. cit.*, testimony of Dr. Klaus Heiss, p. 261.

16. *Hearings*, Part 1,*op. cit.*, p. 1.

17. *Weekly Compilation of Presidential Documents*, The White House,Monday, November 26, 1979 *47*, pp. 2141–2152, emphasis added.

18. *Hearings*, Part 2, *op. cit.*,Dr. Klaus Heiss, p. 261.

19. *Private Sector Involvement In Civil Space Remote Sensing*, prepared by an Interagency Task Force, Washington, D.C., June 15, 1979, *1*, p.1.

20. *Ibid.*,Appendix 5.

21. *Hearings*, Part 1, *op. cit.*, *p.73.*

22. *Private Sector Involvement, op. cit.*, Appendix 7.

23. *Ibid.*, Appendix 5.

24. *Hearings*, Part 1, *op. cit.*, p.72.

25. *Ibid.*, p. 181.

26. *Ibid.*, p. 211.

27. *Ibid.*, pp. 107, 121.

28. *Fox Butterfield* "U.S. plans to sell a satellite ground station to China," *The New York Times*, January 9, 1980, p. A9.

29. *Private Sector Involvement, op. cit.*, Appendix: State and Local Views.

30. *Ibid.*, Appendix 5.

31.   John Howkins, "Remote sensing—Photographing the Earth," *Intermedia*, International Institute of Communications, London, April 1978, *6* (2), p. 8.

32.   Jonathan F. Gunter, Senior Project Director, "The United States and the debate on the world 'information order'," Academy for Educational Development (AED), Washington, D.C., August 1978, p. 98.

33.   R. B. MacDonald & F. G. Hall, "Global crop forecasting," *Science*, May 16, 1980, *208*, pp.670–679.

34.   Gunter, *op. cit.*, p. 23.

35.   Marc U. Porat, "Communication policy in an information society," in *Communications for tomorrow: Policy perspectives for the 1980s*, Glen O. Robinson, Ed., New York: Praeger Publishers, 1978, p. 48.

36.   For an extended and helpful review of the issue of national sovereignty and remote sensing, see: Allan Gottlieb, Charles Dalfen & Kenneth Katz, "The transborder transfer of information by communications and computer systems: Issues and approaches to guiding principles," *American Journal of International Law*, April 1974, *68* (2).

37.   Discussions before the Scientific and Technical sub-committee of the Committee on the Peaceful Uses of Outer Space. Outer Space Scientific and Technical Sub-Committee, Seventeenth Session, 228th meeting, February 4, 1980, Department of Public Information, United Nations, New York.

chapter seven

Who Needs Computer Communications?

The concept behind Clarkson [College's] new library was developed by representatives of the General Electric Company, Xerox, International Business Machines and other major corporations. Dr. Plane [Clarkson's President] said it was the college's decision to bypass academia for advice because 'colleges aren't very good at the future; what we're good at is the past.'

The New York Times, October 21, 1980, p. C1

In 1980 there were 400,000 computers, large and small, operating in the United States.[1] Computer capacity grows annually at an astonishing tempo. Installation proceeds almost as rapidly in some nations in Western Europe. Well behind, but not entirely neglected, communications hardware and systems are being introduced, in varying amounts, in the less industrialized peripheral states.

These trends seem to suggest a universalistic movement, at differential speeds, with the less developed countries following the more industrialized, to computer communications. Implicit in this pattern also seems to be the belief that what is good and useful for

135

some powerful groups in the industrially advanced market economies is equally desirable and helpful to people everywhere.

A review of the functions electronic technology serve in the
United States' economy—still the centerpiece in the world market
system—indicates that this may be a very questionable assumption. It is by no means indisputable that what is required by and
serviceable to the dominant groups in the priviledged core of the
world economic order, is necessary or acceptable in either the out-
lying regions, dependent on and exploited by the center, or in fact,
for the general public in the center itself.

COMPUTERIZATION IN THE U.S. TRANSNATIONAL SYSTEM

A good case can be made for claiming that the world position of
American capitalism increasingly depends on the rapid and
unhindered utilization of computer communications throughout the
economy. The core of the U.S. transnational system essentially
comprises the domestic and international operations of a few thousand powerful super-corporations, their inner ring conveniently
labelled the *Fortune 500*. Separations between foreign and domestic operations of these companies becomes increasingly difficult to
disentangle as their business becomes ever more global.

The same firms, with few exceptions, engage in the world market not only as exporters of goods and services, but also as exporters of capital. There now exists, as a consequence, a privately
owned industrial system, located outside continental boundaries,
which represents more than $200 billion of U.S. corporate capital
invested in plants and facilities. At the same time, an ever growing
component of domestic economic activity is generated directly from
the foreign operations of the super-corporations. This is noticeable
especially, but not exclusively, in the service fields, in which the
United States has become the entrepot for a global empire of commerce, finance, and information handling. Banking, insurance,
property transactions, information—recreational, business, military, and administrative—have become leading activities which facilitate and maintain the global as well as the domestic stakes of the
Fortune 500.

With some room for variation in individual corporate management strategies, the transnational system, interacting continu-

ously with the domestic sphere, is administered centrally by its owners and managers. It is in the performance of these administrative and operational functions that computers have become essential instrumentation for the transnational corporation. The role of computers and telecommunications in the control and management of a modern, globally active company, is described by one prominent corporate official:

> The merging of computer and communications technologies can transform the way in which multinational corporations operate. Today a company can collect data on its operations and personnel from all parts of the world, and almost instantaneously transmit such data to a single location for storage, processing, and further dissemination. This provides the management of these companies with current information for decision-making on a scale never before possible. As a result of these technologically-based breakthroughs new concepts of management are appearing.[2]

The more industrial operations are undertaken internationally by the *Fortune 500*, the larger their requirements for financial and banking services. Stepping forward to supply these services are the powerful American commercial banks. For example, *Bank of America* and *Citicorp* (holding company for *Citibank*) "increased the deposits in their respective overseas branches about $22 billion [over the past five years]. On June 30, 1979, Citicorp's overseas deposits amounted to more than $45 billion and Bank of America's stood at $39 billion. Citicorp now depends on overseas earnings for about 70 percent of its profits, and Bank of America for 50 percent."[3]

These huge sums reflect the magnitude of the financial transactions being undertaken by these organizations. They indicate also the reason for computerizing the operations of these entities. This is confirmed by a top executive of Citibank, the operating company of the Citicorp organization.

> There is no easy way to describe to you the magnitude of the money transactions that banks transmit around the world everyday. Perhaps it is sufficient to say that we are living in an increasingly interdependent world. . . . Today, *Citibank* provides . . . services in over 100 countries. Our operations have taken on a geographic dimension that was not present a couple of decades ago. . . . Today's

high transaction volumes and geographhic spread have introduced communications problems that demand sophisticated technological solutions . . . the complexity of international business today places a premium on speed and accuracy. . . . This is why we are primarily dependent upon electronic media for international communications, both in providing services to our customers and in administrative communication between our branches.[4]

Sophisticated computer communications are important in other applications, as well as in the maintenance of a transational economic order. They are indispensable for transmitting, processing, and distributing the intelligence secured by the numerous sensing ('spy') satellites orbiting the planet.

In addition to surveillance and military communication functions—the global "law and order" machinery of domination[5]—some satellites provide detailed, global natural resource information, which finds its way, directly or circuitously, to the planning staffs of the big mining, oil, and agribusiness corporations.[6] (See Chap. 6).

It hardly needs saying that the informatics needs of transnational corporations, banks, advertising agencies, and the international police forces of imperialism are not quite the same as the needs of nations and peoples who suffer the impacts of what these global actors are doing. The 'interdependencies' these organizations and structures have established in the world economy are grounded in domination. In the same sense, the interdependencies the peripheral economies experience are expressive of their domination.

In this asymmetrical relationship, more developed computerization and telecommunications in the peripheral states cannot be looked upon as liberating. As they would be introduced and operated, hooking the weaker states into webs of unequal associations, they are almost certain guarantors of deepened dependency. Interdependencies, contrary to the assertions of the transnational advocates, may not, and generally are not, mutually beneficial, because power is unevenly distributed in the first place.

COMPUTERIZATION IN THE CENTER OF THE SYSTEM

The United States' private, corporate economy, if it intends to maintain a commanding world position—already seriously challenged—must allow, indeed promote, continuous shifts and changes in the structure and character of its productive functions. The growth of manufacturing capacity in countries until recently nonindustrial, for example, places heavy competitive pressure on the older manufacturing industries at home. The condition is intensified as the transnational companies move their production sites unhesitatingly to the cheapest, most complaisant national territories.

As the domestic foundations of manufacturing crumble under the growing competition from lower cost producers abroad, American capitalism attempts to recoup its losses by vigorously pushing new technologies, especially communications and electronics. The computer manufacturing industry, the microcomputer field, and the data processing and telecommunications industries are seen as providing the best chance for systemic retention of some measure of international control and authority.

Some envision a new world division of labor, in which the United States' "information economy" will supply the managerial and informational needs of the rest of the world—minus Western Europe and Japan. Vincent E. Giuliano, senior consultant with Arthur D. Little, Co., writes:

> Driving the information society are some of the most dynamic high-growth industries in the U.S. today: companies that provide computer equipment—big main-frame systems, mini-systems, peripherals; office automation equipment suppliers, or word processing switching, copier-duplicator, facsimile, microform and other systems; telephone companies, and communications equipment and service suppliers; remote terminal information service and data base access companies; and manufacturers of microcomputers, semiconductors, and "intelligent electronics" of all kinds.
> These are the industries where the U.S. has a technology edge, where it is a major net exporter.[7]

Yet even here there is uncertainty. Already there is widely felt anxiety among U.S. manufacturers over Japanese inroads into one of the most advanced information technology sectors—the microcomputer field.[8]

Still the necessity remains that new markets be found for new goods and new services. These products, it is counted on, will be "information goods." Selling these systems, goods, and services is an imperative for the continued strength and well-being of American capitalism.

There is also determination to hold on to whatever advantages remain in the older, familiar industries—steel, autos, chemicals, food processing, etc. Expectations for long-term profits in these fields demand, it is believed, computerization of work sites as well as clerical, accounting and managerial functions. "Productivity" is the code word in this endeavor to extract a higher output from the labor force. Automated offices, fully equipped with word processing machines, and assembly lines with computerized robots are on the way to becoming standard work environments.

Computerization is regarded as the most up-to-date means, in a long historical procession of mechanization, to achieving an edge in worldwide competition. This, then, is the "race" that American capitalism *must* run, and in which other, less industrialized, economies are persuaded or forced to participate.

For the *Fortune 500*, the majority shareholders in the world business system, the race means holding onto what they already have and, maybe, getting a bit more. For the governing classes in the less developed nations, the race means getting a slightly better cut of the global resource pie. For the working people everywhere, the race means being brought directly into the world system of production which eliminates any possibility of democratic determination of *what* should be produced, *how* it should be produced, and *who* should share in the social product.

RATIONALIZING THE IRRATIONAL: COMPUTERIZATION AS A CURATIVE FOR SYSTEMIC MALADY

Still another strong force promoting computerization in the United States is what might be called rationalizing the high density sector of irrationality in the economy. This, it should be emphasized, is no marginal or secondary component in the system. It derives directly from the structure of production, the role of serving as an imperial entrepot, and the domestic unequal distribution of income.

Some of the elements in this sector are particularly noteworthy, for they focus attention on computer applications that are associated almost entirely with a late capitalist 'model' of development that hardly can claim universality, much less perpetuity.

Table 7.1 presents the annual gross revenues of the major information industries. It is a statistical snapshot of what constitutes the

TABLE 7.1: ANNUAL GROSS REVENUES OF THE MAJOR INFORMATION INDUSTRIES

Information Industries	Approximate Gross Revenue (in billions of dollars)				
	1970	1974	1975	1976	1977
Telephone	18.2	28.3	31.3	35.6	40.8
Telegraph	0.4	0.5	0.5	0.5	0.6
Specialized common carriers	0.0	0.0	0.0	0.1*	0.2*
Satellite carriers	0.1	0.1	0.1	0.2	0.2
Mobile radio systems	2.0	2.9	3.2	3.5	a
Postal service	6.3	9.0	10.0	11.2	13.0
Private information delivery services	0.7†	1.3†	1.6†	1.7†	2.4†
Pulp, paper, and board	13.0†	17.1†	a	a	a
Photographic equipment and supplies	3.9†	6.0†	a	a	a
Radio, TV, and communication equipment	12.8†	16.8†	a	a	a
Electronic components and accessories	12.8†	20.3†	a	a	a
Computer systems manufacturers	b	16.6	18.8	21.1	23.8
Computer software and service suppliers	1.6	3.2	3.8	4.5	5.3
Broadcast television	2.8	3.8	4.1	5.2	5.9
Cable television	0.3	0.6	0.7	1.0	a
Broadcast radio	1.1	1.6	1.7	2.0	a
Motion pictures	3.8	5.5	5.4	a	a
Organized sports, arenas	1.0*†	c	c	c	c
Theaters	1.5	2.5	2.7	a	a
Newspapers and wire services	7.0	9.6	10.5	11.7	13.4*
Periodicals (including newsletters)	3.2	4.1	4.4	5.0*	5.6*
Business consulting services	0.9	1.7	1.8	a	a
Advertising	7.9	9.7	10.0	a	a
Brokerage industries	40.6	64.0	69.1	a	a
Book publishing and printing	3.4	4.5	4.8	5.2	5.6*
Libraries	2.1	d	d	d	d
Schooling	70.1	97.7	110.8	121.4	130.6*
Research and development	25.9	32.7	35.1	38.5	42.7*
Federal information institutions					
Census Bureau	0.1	0.1	0.1	0.1	0.1
National intelligence community	4.0*†	7.0*	10.0*†	6.0 *†	e
NTIS‡	0.0	0.0	0.0	0.0	0.0
Social Security Administration	1.0	1.9	2.2	2.6	2.7
County agents, government	0.3	0.4	0.4	0.5	0.5
		136.2	132.7	a	a
Insurance	92.6	133.1	148.8	a	a
Legal services	8.5	13.7	14.8	a	a

*Estimated. †Lower bound. ‡National information Service.

Symbols: a, government statistics are routinely compiled for this industry but were not yet available for this year; b, industry statistics consistent with those for the following years are not available; c, major league sports are as intimately linked to the television industry as motion picture production and therefore qualify for inclusion. The organizations are, however, generally privately held and, except for a rare special study, data about them are not available; d, statistics are routinely compiled for only some types of libraries; e, figures are not normally released by the government but became available for prior years through congressional hearings.

Source: *Science*, July 4, 1980, *209*, p.1949. Copyright 1980 by the American Association for the Advancement of Science.

"information society" as it has developed in the United States. It is also, and not without reason, the sector where computerization has proceeded most rapidly.

With the exception of schooling, the most important information industries are those most involved with property—its acquisition, transfer and protection. Thus, banking and credit, brokerage, insurance, accounting, legal services, and advertising together account for the bulk of the activities that are designated as 'informational'. In a word, services mostly associated with the socio-legal structure of production and distribution of the *Fortune 500*, at home and abroad, constitute the sphere most involved with computerization. It is a sphere that might be greatly reduced in an alternate social formation.

The line that divides useful from wasteful work is hard to draw, though some fine theoretical distinctions have been applied over time in attempts to do so. One interesting effort contrasts paper and product entrepreneurs. Paper entrepreneurs, according to Robert Reich, are

> Trained in law, finance, accountancy—manipulate complex systems of rules and numbers. They innovate by using the system in novel ways: establishing joint ventures, consortiums, holding companies, mutual funds; finding companies to acquire, 'white knights' to be acquired by, commodity futures to invest in, tax shelters to hide in; engaging in proxy fights, tender offers, antitrust suits, stock splits, spinoffs, divestitures; buying and selling notes, bonds, convertible debentures, sinking fund debentures; obtaining Government subsidies, loan guarantees, tax breaks, contracts, licences, quotas, price supports, bail-outs; going private, going public, going bankrupt.[10]

Stock market operations, real estate transactions, personal financial transactions with credit cards, individual insurance, and advertising are some of the most prominent forms of computer-facilitated paper entrepreneurialism. Consider, for example, an account which makes the case for computerization of the New York Stock Exchange:

> Aided by a trend toward large-sized orders, the exchange recently handled 81.6 million shares, well above the 16.4 million shares traded on October 29, 1929, the Black Tuesday of market history. In its bluntest terms, however, the question is how and to what extent a huge computer will replace the paper-littered trading floor and the

2,500 men and women who form the core of the country's stock markets . . . the electronic age has begun, says Donald Regan, chairman of Merrill Lynch & Company, which owns the nation's largest and most highly automated brokerage firm. "Now is the time for the exchange to accept electronics more, to become more productive."[11]

Eugene Garfield, one of the founders of the Information Industry Association, regards developments such as these as a strong indication of the rising information consciousness of the American people: "Stockbrokers now take for granted rapid electronic access to market quotations. . . . This is an area of human endeavor that was practically untouched by the computer just a decade ago. The information consciousness of the people in this industry is characteristic of what we can expect in the society of the future."[12] It is evident that "the society of the future" is assumed to include stock quotations.

Life insurance offers another shining example of the utility of computerization in an industry which is a private enterprise activity and requires massive clerical operations, at least some of which might be reduced with another mode of societal protection. *Business Week* reports on the growth of computerization in this sector:

> Most of the larger life companies, for example made huge cost savings in the past ten years by computerizing policy handling and other headquarters activities. Kemper Life Insurance Co., for one, was able to reduce the ratio of employees to new sales by 1977 to just one-fifteenth of what it had been in 1972.[13]

Not just the large insurance companies are being automated. A similar process is beginning to occur with the individual life insurance agents, the independents who sell the policies. Up to now, "only a few hundred of the nation's more than 70,000 independent agents have installed even limited data processing hookups with their insurance companies. . . . The industry, however, is beginning to realize its inefficiency in communicating with its agents."[14]

The irony of reducing inefficiency in the operations of an industry which is itself the embodiment of a systemic inefficiency—the handling on an individual basis of a social necessity, insurance—is breathtaking. Computerization appears as a 'solution' to an institutional arrangement which is obsolete to begin with.

Some of the other fields which reveal similar characteristics of systemic resource misuse are real estate, banking, market research, and advertising. The millions of real estate transactions which arise from the private ownership of land, its sale and resale, and the financial and accounting transactions involved in these multitudinous deals, are obviously facilitated with computers. Banks alone, according to one estimate, "process 8.5 billion pieces of information a year."[15] So too, the huge direct mail advertising campaigns undertaken to sell goods, services, political candidates, and programs are increasingly dependent on computerization.

AMI (Advertising and Marketing Intelligence), described as "the data base whose time has come," is made available by *The New York Times* Information Service. It illustrates the special benefits computerization offers to certain kinds of information seekers:

> In seconds, the system provides data in answer to questions like these: What sort of tasting panels is Wendy's using to compete with McDonald's? How much has Perrier's ad budget increased during its recent successful U.S. marketing effort? Who is now handling the ITT account? Is the life insurance industry running into any regulatory problems? What is the demograhic outlook for household detergents and soap in the 1980's? What were the details of the most recent Nielsen study on cable TV reach?[16]

The number of economic activities utilizing electronic technology is multiplying. The examples cited above and the fields involved are associated with the particular features of capitalism and its growth. But it is evident also that the onrush of computerization *in general* in the United States is inextricably tied to the kind of economic and social activities generated overall by the economy. Seen from this perspective, the dynamics of the system itself *compel* the introduction of advanced electronic calculation.

If this is indeed the case, the central question is more relevant than ever. It inquires, Just how useful is the American 'model' for other societies, which may still have options for deciding their patterns of existence? In fact, the question may be directed inward. How useful is the model for the United States itself, faced with new global circumstances that make resource misuse an ever-deepening source of crisis?

Asking questions such as these is not the same as arguing that computerization is socially useless and maybe destructive. No grounds exist for such a condemnation. What is at issue is the systemic development and utilization of computer power to facilitate an economic order which is inherently exploitative and wasteful of human and natural resources, domestically and internationally. This order, at the same time, possesses tremendous power and is remarkably capable of attracting and pulling other countries and peoples into the orbit of its operations. It is in this context that challenges to computerization are raised.

It is precisely to head off such challenges and deflect such questions that the wondrous capabilities of modern communication technologies are prominently publicized. As we have seen, there is little question but that electronic communications are of vital importance to the transnational corporate scheme of things. The aim of American policy, however, is to make scores of poor, weak, and dependent nations believe that what is of great utility to supercorporations also holds the answer to their own, quite different needs.

Roland Homet, director of the U.S. International Communication Agency's (ICA) Office of International Communications Policy, expresses this position nicely. Many countries, he says, "are succumbing to reactionary impulses to restrict the free flow of information by trying to limit the sophistication of international telecommunications systems." To prevent this, Homet recommends that "The U.S. must educate the international community in the importance of telecommunications technology to national development." Homet believes that "senior management of U.S. industry is the group best suited to lead that educational campaign and force the isssue into the highest political councils."[17]

IBM Director of data security, standards, and product safety, L. J. Rankine, assumes this 'educational role' and assures the representatives of 60 nations gathered at an Intergovernmental Bureau of Informatics (IBI) international meeting in Rome in June 1980, that "Informatics is capable of helping every nation to reach higher levels of economic, social and cultural benefit, if properly harnessed and directed."[18]

The adoption of the latest information technologies, runs the argument, will permit the less developed world to leapfrog into modernity. Modern communication technology will make it easier for poor nations to "catch up"—the race, again—with the advanced, select few. Otherwise, it is noted lugubriously, the passage on the way to development will be lengthy, painful, and insecure.

A detailed program, advanced by the president of the British Computing Society, is representative of this thinking. Proposing the formation of a Council for the Application of Computer Technology for Development, the Council would undertake these tasks:

1.   Assign British nationals to advise and assist with the establishment of government policies and plans.
2.   Establish curricula courses of instruction and examination structures
3.   Provide educational facilities in the UK for students from developing countries
4.   Plan and create technical training facilities
5.   Prepare training materials, technical manuals and teaching aids.
6.   Assist in the creation of a professional structure
7.   Assist in the planning and creation of a National Computing Center
8.   Organize technical seminars and conferences
9.   Assist in the definition and implementation of strategic projects.[19]

This program, which is typical of past U.S. initiatives, however well-meaning the intentions of its author, could easily be regarded as a blueprint for the longlasting dependence of any society that participated in it. Material dependence on equipment, parts, servicing, and management is built into the relationship. Though it might diminish over time, it is more likely to increase with each new technological development produced in the UK, or whichever core country established the program.

A more longlasting dependence would accompany the non-material factors in the 'assistance' design. The education, values, and professionalization of local cadres in the newly established informatics system are to be patterned on the training and instruction offered by the center of expertise, UK in the proposed instance.

Just as many of the English ex-colonies have their indigenous mini-BBCs (adopted models of UK broadcasting), the computer age if recommendations like these are accepted, will see the growth of national computer systems structured, administered, and directed toward objectives no different from those operating in the advanced centers. Additionally, and more threatening still to national sovereignty, these indigenous systems will be integrated into those in the center, providing thereby the circuits and processing instrumentation for further integration of the economies in general. Once this occurs, it will be advanced as conclusive 'proof' of the necessity for 'interdependence'.

The President of the British Computing Society concedes much of this at the outset. He acknowledges that even if his recommendations are adopted and a major effort mounted by a participating state, its dependency will not be overcome:

> It seems likely that the technology gap can never be bridged. The cost of setting out on a technological development path and catching up with the world leaders would be outside the capability of practically any nation.[20]

So the race which the developing countries are continually invited or pressured to join can't be won by them in any case. Yet entering the race serves a purpose. It fixes the participant into an enduring relationship of dependence. Here too, the British Computing Society's president is forthright:

> This does not mean a country should not attempt to carve out a particular area of technological leadership, but there must in the future always be some major dependence upon the most advanced nations.[21]

WHAT TO DO WITH COMPUTER COMMUNICATIONS: A FEW CONSIDERATIONS

One writer, reviewing current developments in computerization and transborder data flows, concluded: "There is no reason to believe that the trend toward increasing interconnections and interdependence among countries, especially as evidenced in steadily more powerful telecommunications facilities, will be reversed in the foreseeable future. . . . It seems evident that a large part of the increase can be attributed to business use, for both verbal and data communication."[22]

The evidence to date supports this assessment, but one important qualification should be added. The growth of transnational computer communications and the 'interdependence' they create are not predestined nor irreversible world tendencies. They are historically and systemically connected to the prevailing structures of world business enterprise. The world business system, thriving as it appears to be under transnational management, cannot be regarded as a permanent fixity of international economic relationships. It is currently the dominant mode; its longevity is another matter entirely. Some developments indicate that the life expectancy of the world business system may be briefer than its present state of health would seem to suggest.

Among the developments which may affect the future character of the world economy and considerably lessen, if not eliminate, over time the influence of the transnational corporations is the appearance of national policy making as a chosen instrument for sovereign decision making.

National policy formation carries no guarantees of rationality, social utility, or even opposition to the now dominant world system of transnational enterprise. What social group(s) has (have) control of the state heavily determines the character of the policies that are formulated.

Still, national policy making *of any kind* creates an awareness of issues and relationships that previously may have been buried under a seemingly 'natural order'. Once issues appear on an overt, public agenda, the protective veil of implicitness is torn off. The lack of knowledgability that permits certain power relationships to exist unquestioned is at least partly overcome. Sooner or later, thereafter, challenges may be expected.

In international affairs, the last 20 years have seen a growth of awareness across a very wide range of social, economic, and cultural matters. Movements for a new international economic order and a new international information order, the protracted international meetings over a "law of the sea" covenant, and the debates over the uses of outer space testify to widespread and increasing efforts to throw open for discussion and to change innumerable areas hitherto under accepted Western and corporate control.

Though little has been achieved to date in changing exploitative economic, cultural, and informational relationships between the powerful and the weak, the documentation and knowledgability of the mechanics of these relationships have been set forth amply in countless international sessions, resolutions, papers and studies.[23]

The markers have been set down against which to measure future behavior and action. Also, in the acts of documentation, consciousness of conditions has been broadened and internationalized. In this sense, a different sort of interdependence, one shaped from mutual deprivation and exploitation, is perceived in many parts of the world.

Withal, the installation of new communication technology and its utilization to serve transnational corporate requirements does not yet encounter either widespread, unified or determined opposition (See Chap. 8.) The movement towards computerization, along the lines set down in the transnational centers, proceeds.

The movement, and the problems it engenders, may be unresolvable for the time being. This is so largely because of the massive inequality in economic power between nations and groups within nations. Thus, even when attention is drawn to likely negative developments accompanying computerization, the momentum and weight of established economic power pushes the movement forward.

International organizations such as UNESCO, The Intergovernmental Bureau of Informatics (IBI), the United Nations itself, and other related bodies mention the need for and sometimes encourage the creation of programs for safeguarding national sovereignty and autonomy in the field of information. Having done this, they feel satisfied that computer communications can proceed and actually serve social needs in nations at all levels of development. Yet the present worldwide constellation of economic and technological power envelops these programs and transforms their protective character into mechanisms for undermining the sovereignty they were designed to safeguard.

It appears, therefore, that something more than protective international rulemaking—useful as this is as an indication of awareness—is required to safeguard more effectively the social development of most of the world. What is called for, at this stage in international existence, is a maximum effort directed as slowing down, and postponing wherever possible, the rush to computerization. New technology moratoria, of the sort the Australian Council on Trade Union Policy proposed in 1979,[24] which recommended a five year moratorium, offer, at minimum, an opportunity for evaluation and consideration of the consequences and impact of the new computerization on existing social structures and human well-being.

Temporization may seem to be a timid, if not unrealistic stance in a 'new age'. Perhaps the 'new age' itself needs evaluation. Does each country require a growing sector of computerized irrationality? Do the interdependencies that presently organized global transmission systems, data banks, and transborder data flows create, promote or distort national development? One development officer notes, for example, "by far the most important type of information, both in volume and value to any one country, is the locally produced information."[25] Imported information, on the other hand, may often be irrelevant, inappropriate, or unadaptable. This is equally true for technology and education as it is for information.

Deliberateness on behalf of maintaining social autonomy requires no apology—especially when precipitate action is the recommendation of those seeking to perpetuate or extend domination. The conclusions in the 1980 Final Report of the International Commission for the Study of Communication Problems (McBride Commission), on technological innovation are well worth reflection:

> Technological innovations open up vast new possibilities. However, a word of caution is necessary: they are not instant miracles, but tools to be introduced and used only after careful consideration is given to all possible resulting ramifications. Each has particular potential, yet none is an isolated means; they are parts of a total system, which should be planned and shaped bearing in mind the integration of all its parts. Technological innovations can often have negative effects, both economic and social, and may distort directions and priorities for overall development activities. However inviting, introduction of some new technologies should be seriously considered, *and perhaps delayed*, in certain developmental situations. It must also be remembered that introduction of new technologies is often easier than subsequent provision of software required for their optimum utilization. . . . Caution is further advised because of the fact that the control of the production and utilization of these information processing and telecommunication systems is at present mainly in the hands of industrialized countries and, in some instances, of a few transnational companies. The implications of this situation for worldwide social and economic development—and, in particular, the installation of a New International Economic Order—require the attention of the international community as a whole.[26]

Slowing down, if not halting, the installation of computer communications now will not of itself produce optimal conditions for their eventual application at a later time. Yet it does hold open such a possibility.

To make the most of this opportunity, a go-slow policy for informatics requires, at the same time, the beginning of a systematic and comprehensive international effort to develop standards, codes, and conditions of applicability *before* computerization is introduced into any locale. As there are differing public and private, national and international interests, such standards and codes will not be promulgated quickly. This is all to the good. It will afford time to think through the enormous complexities that surround advanced communication and other technologies at this stage of unequal global power and influence.

Notes to Chapter Seven

1. Jake Kirchner, "'Nazi techniques' envisioned for DP security," *Computerworld*, April 14, 1980, p. 14.

2. Hugh P. Donaghue, vice president of Control Data Corporation, "The business community's stake in global communications," paper delivered at the 43rd Annual Meeting of the U.S. National Commission for UNESCO, Athens, Georgia, December 12, 1979.

3. Robert A. Bennett, "Bank America, Citicorp near $100 billion," *The New York Times*, September 24, 1979, p.D1.

4. Robert B. White, *International Communication & Information*, Hearings before the subcommittee on International Operations of the Committee on Foreign Relations, United States Senate, 95th Congress, First Session, June 10, 1977, U.S. GPO, Washington, D.C., 1977, pp. 246–251.

5. Dr. John McLucas, executive vice president, Comsat Corporation, Hearings before the Subcommittee on Science, Technology, and Space of the Committee on Commerce, Science and Transportation, United States Senate, 96th Congress, First Session, on S.663 and S.875, Part 1, April 9 & 11, 1979, pp. 208–209. Dr. McLucas testified: "Specifically, the reason for carrying out Defense Department Collection [of data] activities is to be prepared for some kind of a military contingency, or to know more about what adversaries are doing."

6. *Ibid.*

7. Vincent E. Giuliano, "'Rear-view' vision limits growth," *Information World*, March 1980, *2*(11).

8. *Datamation*, April 1980, p. 168.

9.   Anthony G. Oettinger, "Information resources: Knowledge and power in the 21st century," *Science*, July 4, 1980, *209*, pp. 191–198.

10.   Robert B. Reich, "Entrepreneurialism," *The New York Times*, May 23, 1980, A31.

11.   Karen W. Arensen, "New York Stock Exchange faces challenge," *The New York Times*, October 29, 1979, p. A1.

12.   Eugene Garfield, "2001: An information society," Institute for Scientific Information, Philadelphia, Pa., June 23, 1979.

13.   "The coming crunch in life insurance," *Business Week*, December 3, 1979, p.125.

14.   "Insurance agents go electronic," *Businesss Week*, November 19, 1979, p. 42.

15.   Marcy Rosenberg, "Americans see DP power as 'Big Brother': Goldwater," *Computerworld*, April 21, 1980, p. 13.

16.   "Announcing an advertising and marketing break-through," advertisement, *The New York Times*, April 30, 1980, p. A16.

17.   "Privacy trend 'ominous'," *Computerworld*, November 12, 1979, p. 34.

18.   Jake Kirchner, "IBM, Cbema urge restraint in data flow laws," *Computerworld*, June 30, 1980, p. 10.

19.   Rex Malik, "What kind of DP help for developing nations?", *Computerworld*, March 17, 1980, p. 37.

20.   *Ibid.*

21.   *Ibid..*

22.   Richard H. Veith, "Informatics and transborder data flow: The question of social impact," *Journal of the American Society for Information Science*, March 1980, *31* (2), p. 109.

23.   United Nations' and associated international agencies' documentation overflow depository libraries. More recently, the reports and proceedings of the Non-Aligned Nations, the European, African, Asian, and Latin American regional associations, add to a volume of information that can hardly be systematically recorded. A recent example in the information field are the reports and monographs—more than a hundred—of the International Commission for the Study of Communication Problems (The McBride Commission), UNESCO, Paris, 1979 & 1980.

24.   Susan Coleman, "Australian workers seeking voice in technological changes," *Computerworld*, August 20, 1979, p.1.

25.   H. M. Woodward, "Future information requirements of the Third World," *Journal of Information Science*, 1980, *1* pp. 259–265.

26.   *Many Voices, One World*, report by the International Commission for the Study of Communication Problems, Kogan Page, London/Unipub, New York/UNESCO, Paris, 1980, p. 95, emphasis added.

chapter eight

The Insecure Foundations of the *Fortune 500's* Information Age

In my personal view, computers are job killers and the sooner we accept this, the sooner we will start to deal with the implications effectively.

Calvin C. Gotlieb, "Computers—A gift of fire," International Federation for Information Processing's (Ifip) Congress 80, Tokyo, October 1980.

PROSPECTS FOR U.S. DOMINATION OF A NEW INTERNATIONAL DIVISION OF LABOR

Computerization of the American economy is being propelled by a combination of factors and pressures. Some of these are: the hope to maintain or restore a competitive edge in manufacturing; the need to compensate for an unfavorable balance of trade with exports of information products and services; the utility of electronic communication to the world-spanning operations of the U.S.-based and owned transnational corporations; the profitable application of accumulated technological know-how, derived from decades of enormous military and military-related expenditures on research and development; and the necessity to 'rationalize' a swollen, low productivity sector of service activities which has attended the growth of an advanced, capitalist economy.

Electronic communication and computerization, in this context, are seen as vitalizing forces, allowing some to believe that the century looming may be the genuine American Century, arriving only fifty years later than Henry Luce predicted it would. For example, John Eger, former head of telecommunications policy in the Nixon Administration, confidently states: "Our influence, whether purposefully channeled or not, is likely to increase during the rest of the century."[1]

Pleasant as this prospect of renewed authority and profitability may be to certain sectors of American leadership, there are numerous barriers that stand in the way of its fulfillment. A new international division of labor, which allows corporate America to handle most of the world's information generation, processing, and distribution, has to take into account at least three major sources of actual and potential opposition. These are: the rivalry of other developed, market economies; the Third (Non-Aligned, less developed, etc.) World and its claims and demands on the industrialized West; and an uncertain and volatile domestic situation, which at almost any moment could produce far-reaching and incalculable political and economic shifts.

Not without effect also, but not examined here, is the impact, if any, of the socialist sector of the world economy on the development of a new international division of labor. It seems reasonably clear that in the years immediately ahead, the socialist grouping will be more reactive than initiatory. Increasingly pulled into the international market economy, this sector is paradoxically more likely to act as a stabilizer than as a source of disequilibrium in the world market economy.

(1) The Competition of Western Europe and Japan

Bertram Gross argues that one of the major accomplishments of American capitalism in the 35 year interval since World War II has been its ability to overcome serious rivalries and disagreements *inside* the world capitalist system, and to establish a general solidary front of previously warring factions.[2] To a certain extent, this achievement has been the unintentional outcome of the dominant position of U.S. capitalism in the early postwar period. As the Western European and Japanese economies rebuilt and expanded their industrial systems, the antagonisms of competing coalitions of private economic power have resurfaced. Still, what Gross and others have called the "golden international"—the global interlocks of capital—manages to maintain unity in the face of the worldwide workers' movement. But fissures are beginning to appear.

With the rapid development of computer communications, and the accelerated movement toward a new international division of labor they promote, there is recognition that a totally new dimension of cultural and economic control has emerged—one that threatens developed as well as less developed economies—and therefore, developed as well as less developed capitalist groupings. One expression of this recognition appears in a 1979 study prepared for the Commission of the European Communities. The report notes:

> Control over the "telematics system" as a whole is slipping away from Europe to an ever-increasing extent. It will be some time before the ground lost in the large computer field, where 76% of the market is held by American firms, is made up.

Unless major corrective actions are taken, the study warns, "domination of the telematics industry by the United States and Japan would, in the more or less short run, result in:

- The final loss of European control over an essential field;
- Damage to the competitive position of the Community, both in Europe and in the rest of the world;
- The loss of the potential new jobs, which should compensate for loss of jobs caused by the new technologies;
- *A reduction in our independence in decision-making in all walks of public and private life.*"[3]

In Japan too, hard as it may be to imagine, there is anxiety over the American data base companies operating there. An official of the Nippon Telegraph and Telephone Public Corporation (NTT), for example, referring to the penetration these firms have already made in the United Kingdom where they overshadow the English services, expressed fear that "the Japanese data base market [too] might become colonized.[4]

The rapidly unfolding computer-communications era offers rich economic prizes—to say nothing of ideological domination—to those who can seize them. Sales of hardware (computers and related equipment) have received most attention to date, but computer services, the processing and enriching of raw data, increasingly are becoming large scale, lucrative operations, and will become more so in the future. Already in 1978, users in Western Europe spent $5.7 billion for computer services. These have been averaging an annual growth rate of 15%.[5] By 1983, it is estimated that the U.S. and the Western European markets will each approach $12 billion in annual sales of these services.[6] European and Japanese efforts to capture, or at least share in the economic returns to information activity, as well as to avoid a state of informational dependency, have taken two main directions. One, which is followed in most industrially developed countries, has been to strengthen the national capacity to produce, process, and transmit information. These functions can be aggregated into what may be called the *production* side of the competition. On the other side of these efforts, parallel measures have been taken on an individual country and also regional basis to limit and reduce United States information industries' activities in European and Japanese markets. These policies have direct economic consequences but they have been formulated generally in *legal* and *juridical* terms.

On the *production* side, it is already evident that hopes for an unchallenged American worldwide monopoly of the new information technology are unrealizable. Informational developments in France, for example, demonstrate this. A country with an entrepreneurial class deeply sensitive to maintaining an influential position in Europe as well as exerting dominion in Francophone Africa, France, in 1978, outlined the importance of the new information technology in the Presidentially commissioned Nora-Minc Report.[7]

In the same year, the Government adopted the first plan for the actual informatisation of society.[8] Specific programs for promoting national capabilities to produce informatics hardware and software were initiated. Since 1966, the French Government has spent about $1.5 billion to support the data processing industry in general, and the Compagnie Internationale pour L'informatique Honeywell Bull (CIIHB) in particular. In 1978 alone, this company received $1 billion in government contracts. Additionally, the Government is spending substantial amounts to foster the mini, peripherals, and components sectors of the industry. Looking into the future, more than $500 million have been allocated to new data processing applications with special emphasis on introducing computer methods and skills into the French school system. In the fall of 1980, the French Government announced a five-year, $24 billion investment plan in telecommunications and computer technology.[9]

In the French analysis, perhaps more than anywhere else, there is a broad understanding of the vital control points of a modern information system. This is especially evident in the Nora Minc Report's succinct evaluation of the necessity for creating *national* data banks, rather than relying on the already great data depositories that have been created in the United States. Nora and Minc state simply that "data are inseparable from their organization, their mode of storage. In the long run, it is not a question only of the advantage which may be conferred by familiarity with such a datum. The *knowledge will end up by being modeled, as it always has been, on data stores.* Leaving to others—i.e., to American banks— the responsibility for organizing the "collective memory" while being content to dig into it, is the equivalent of accepting cultural alienation. Installing data banks thus constitutes an imperative of sovereignty."[10]

Software development, too, is being heavily supported in France at the governmental level. National data base production is regarded as a high priority objective. The target for 1983 is 50 new data bases.[11]

Though the French are the most visible and active in the European information production race, the entire West European Community now regards the information industries as vital and in urgent need of support. The Commission of the European Communities, for example, "has launched a major initiative aimed at cornering over one third of the world telematics market by 1990."[12] This would include telecommunications systems; computers; semiconductors; software; micro-circuits (chips); data bases. Whether or not these goals are realized, the thrust is clear. United States' industrial dominance in information technology is the target.*

---

*A word of qualification is required. The struggle for market shares and national position, already engaged, frequently is affected in ways difficult to determine by the interlocks, agreements, and understandings of the transnational companies, which have their interests distributed across many national borders. For this reason, what appears as a European or national initiative, often is a well-concealed transnational corporate action or maneuver.

All the same, U.S. officials are very unhappy with recent developments. For example, a staff report of the Committee on Government Operations (96th Congress, 2d Session), December 11, 1980, page 35, concluded: "The EC [European Community] appears committed to an aggressive course of action which could have disturbing ramifications for United States enterprises."

While the Western European industrial region is, for the most part, still organizing its production challenge to American informational technology, the Japanese offensive is well underway. Though there is no Japanese equivalent to IBM, the inroads Japanese electronics products have made into Western and U.S. markets have been striking. Consumer electronics goods have for some time been a preserve of Japanese exports. Now, attention is being focused on the most advanced, high technology sector of the information industries: the microcircuits which supply the core of computerization.

"On a worldwide basis," a *Science* correspondent reports, "American companies' current [1980] share of the semiconductor market (just over two-thirds) is of concern because it has been slowly dropping since the beginning of the integrated circuit era in the early 1960's, when it was 88 percent."[13]

On another front too, the Japanese are creating problems for the U.S. information industry. In 1978, Charles Lecht noted,

> The Japanese computer industry, through the increase of its exports to Germany, is helping to reduce Germany's still heavy dependence on U.S.-owned industry . . . . The introduction of Japanese systems to Germany through Siemens, while not increasing Germany's home-owned computer industry growth, serves to diminish Germany's dependence upon the U.S., such dependence amounting to 72% in the small to large general-purpose systems arena in 1976. Accordingly, the domination of the Western European computer systems market place by U.S. companies, amounting to over 75%, will diminish too.[14]

Confirming Lecht's fear that Japanese competitive intervention in West Germany will lessen American control there, a West German move to discourage the purchase of an American computer in favor of a Siemens' machine, manufactured in Japan by Fijitsu, was reported in the fall of 1980. "American trade officials and computer industry officials have sharply criticized the decision," *The New York Times* reports, "fearing the precedent will damage United States computer sales in West Germany, the American industry's strongest European market, and ironically, open the door to Japanese competition."[15]

These too, are trends which could, possibly, be reversed or overcome, but they add up to increased pressure on America's worldwide position. Moreover, the struggle for command and advantage in the international sphere is unlikely to diminish. "Revitalization of industry" may be an American objective of the 1980s, but its fulfillment lies beyond U.S. will and determination alone.

Production, however, constitutes but one element in the competition. Alongside governmental efforts to promote national capabilities in information technology and production, there are also national and regional attempts to reduce greatly, perhaps eventually exclude, the U.S. information industries' international operations. These efforts are embodied in national and regional policies and are expressed generally as legal covenants and laws seemingly far removed from economic considerations. Thus, the protection of personal privacy (in informational matters) has been one of the salient objectives of European policy making. The issue appears to be the protection of individual rights from computer operations and data processing activities that could take advantage of privileged access to personal data.

The problem is not an imaginary one. There is no question that the individual's protection against bureaucratic computer power, private or governmental, is a deeply felt need and a highly legitimate sphere for legal intervention. Acknowledging this, however, is not to disregard other, no less powerful, motivations at work in the matter of personal privacy.

U.S. business leadership is well aware of the less acknowledgeable implications of the individual privacy protection laws being drafted in Western Europe and elsewhere. The vice president of the Manufacturers Hanover Trust Co., for example, asks:

> What is the true issue? If problems exist and are as serious as some would have us believe, let's identify them for what they are . . . Or are these arguments [of the Europeans] being advanced for political reasons while masking ulterior national motives? . . . Is the real concern protection for host country industries, neutralization of foreign competition? . . . Is the intent to hold international communications users to ransom in the name of transborder data flows in order to increase domestic communications or tax revenue?[16]

Similarly, the Assistant U.S. Trade Representative for Policy Development, in April 1980, informed a Congressional subcommittee on Government Information and Individual Rights:

> Government restrictive actions taken for privacy or technical telecommunications reasons are, in some cases, affecting sales op-

portunities. In many of these cases one has the suspicion that the real purpose for imposing the restriction is a commercial one, in effect to keep U.S. companies from developing a market for information and communications-related services. The potential ramifications of these actions are immense, extending far beyond data and communication services. Not only would U.S. trade in these services diminish, but sales in communications and computer hardware would decline as well. Further, the ability of American multinationals to conduct business operations would be severely hampered.[17]

Actually, the legal-political response of Western European capitalism to American informational supremacy has been developing since the first public, intergovernmental discussions about transborder data flows occurred in Vienna, in September 1977, under the sponsorship of the Organization for Economic Cooperation and Development (OECD).

More an informational forum and an exchange of views than an international conference to set policy, the tone of the meeting revealed strongly divergent national economic interests. This was all the more remarkable because the OECD long has been regarded as, and continues to be, an instrumentality heavily influenced by U.S. views and policies.*

In the same sense, the views of the Swedish representative to the conference were unexpectedly jarring to the Americans present:

Many people at this Symposium seem to think that data protection laws will be a threat to the principle of a free flow of information. There does not seem to be anything free of charge about computerized data banks and the communications systems which collect and disperse information these days. The technologies which are making possible the important advances in all our countries come to us at a certain cost—economic as well as social.[18]

More bluntly still, a French participant felt the information situation in Europe raised these questions:

*"First of all, we are a very active participant in the activities of the OECD," wrote the U.S. Deputy Assistant Secretary of State for Advanced and Applied Technology. "As a matter of fact, I would say that the United States has played a leadership role in the OECD." Hearings before the House of Representatives' Subcommittee on Commerce, October 6, 1977.

(i) Is it thinkable that all material and instruments to aid decision-making should ultimately be accessible, under valid computer access and transmission conditions, at American processing centres only?

(ii) May not the effect of such a monopoly be to impose assumptions, premises, results and hence, indirectly, choices?

(iii) How should one regard the fact that the only computer-accessible models enabling a subscriber to follow European ecoonomic trends are developed in the United States (sometimes by Europeans), the results being distributed through American service companies?[19]

Largely in reaction to these views, postmortems on the Vienna Symposium in the United States were sober and reflective. the State Department officer assigned to the subject area made this analysis of the meeting:

The voices of competition and accommodation with the U.S. have been the prevailing ones in the past. They are still strong. but they are not as prevalent today as in the past, and at Vienna a new tone was becoming evident. The views of the economic nationalists are converging with those of the idealists seeking redress from the problems of the modern computer system.[20]

Hearings on transborder data flow regulation, before a subcommittee of the House of Representatives' Committee on Interstate and Foreign Commerce, were held immediately after the symposium. A background paper prepared for the hearings went to the heart of the issue, as understood from an American corporate perspective:

Serious economic implications are based on seemingly innocuous and reasonably enlightened motivations. American observers discern that they may be mere pretexts to shut out extraterritorial companies. This situation has been labeled as the first skirmish of an "information war." In this view, barriers are aimed explicitly at American companies, since they take up the lion's share of foreign revenues in information technology and expertise. It is observed that modern data communications is threatening to eat into the business of public utilities, as well as private vendors. With the institutional and political strength they can muster, they can force the invoking of sovereign powers. This could also be aimed at American multinational users whose dominance in certain industries such as hotel management and banking make foreign governments uncomfortable. One

American observer notes that commercial development may create a future lucrative market in various countries for selling information resources at a premium to under-developed countries.[21]

What the deeper structural meaning of transborder data flow control involved was supplied by another analysis: According to this appraisal, the data protection regulations Europeans were insisting on at Vienna served "to constrain the rapid growth of U.S.-based time sharing services . . . and information services in Europe. Another use would be to constrain somewhat the control the multinational companies have over their foreign subsidiaries (and thus possibly constrain the spread of these multinationals). And other possible use of data protection would be to limit somewhat the amount of advertising that can be directed to residents of other countries."[22]

The Vienna Symposium was a foretaste of what has happened since. In less than three years, by mid-1980, 24 countries, most but not all in Europe, either have passed data protection legislation or are in some preparatory stage of doing so.

In the same interval, OECD "Guidelines Governing the Protection of Transborder Data Flows of Personal Data," and a Council of Europe "Convention for the Protection of Individuals with regard to Automatic Processing of Personal Data," have been moving slowly toward adoption, each the subject of intense scrutiny and debate, reflecting the participating countries' concern over the stakes involved and their insistence on protecting national information industry interests.

One study of the data protection laws already passed, and a review of the provisions of those in preparation, made this assessment of their potential impact. The legislation is regarded as 'precedent-setting' because it:

- "Is a model for the regulation of all types of legislation.
- "Legitimizes disclosure of company records under close government supervision.
- "Opens security procedures, permits authorities to force changes, permits inspection of computer rooms and gives government access to information about operations.
- "Allows employees to testify before government bodies relieved of company confidentiality rules.
- "Makes data flows of multinationals and their vulnerability to scrutiny by governments of host countries, highly visible.

TABLE 8.1: STATUS OF DATA PROTECTION LEGISLATION,
MAY 1980

Country	National	Sub-National	Reports
Australia		L	RP
Austria	L		R
Belgium	(P)		
Canada	L	L	R
Denmark	L		R
Finland			
France	L		R
Germany	L	L,P	R
Greece			
Iceland			RP
Ireland			
Italy			R
Japan			RP
Luxembourg	L		
Netherlands	(P)		R
New Zealand	L		
Norway	L		R
Portugal	C,(P)		
Spain	C		R
Sweden	L		R
Switzerland		L	RP
United Kingdom			R
United States	L,P	L	R
Yugoslavia			RP

Code::
L = Law Adopted
R = Government Report Prepared
C = Constitutional Provision
P = Legislation in Parliament
(P) = Draft Legislation Prepared
RP = Government Report in Preparation

Transnational Data Report, June 1980, *3*(2).

- "Potentially compromises proprietary information for companies in pharmaceuticals, chemicals, petroleum and advertising by exposure of testing or marketing practices.
- "Forces or blocks some multinationals from some cross-border transfers or corporate data."[23]

Whether these considerable limitations on the operations of the transnational companies actually will be imposed, or whether their potential restrictiveness will be relaxed, U.S. corporate business in Europe cannot fail to feel constrained in its practices and prospects.

These developments do not, of themselves, signify that the unity of Western capitalism in the postwar period is coming to an end. They do indicate that the strains on that unity are multiplying rapidly.

(2) Responses from the Third World

It is evident that the industrially developed market economies have no intention of acceding to an American global information hegemony. How may other countries, outside the Western European-Japanese core area of world capitalism, be expected to respond to their not-yet-fixed assignments in a new world international division of labor, and its informational component in particular?

Clearly, no uniform response could characterize 125 or more countries that comprise the not-so-industrialized world. Reactions are mixed, complicated by contradictory forces, and, therefore, frequently ambiguous. At one and the same time, American efforts toward domination are welcomed and rebuffed, are offered opportunities and presented with difficulties and demands.

Most of the attention and energy in the less developed (Third) world are still concentrated on combatting the conventional patterns of information-cultural domination. The meetings and conferences of these countries over the last decade have focused mostly on Western monopolization of new flows, with some concern expressed also for the direction, amount, and character of TV program and film exports, book publishing and, in some cases, tourism. The preoccupation has been largely with *visible* media products and services, which have, for the most part, streamed out of a few Western sources, mostly the United States, and flooded the rest of the world.

Third World recognition of what has been occurring in electronic information generation and transmission is still at an early stage. This in no way, however, minimizes the level of awareness and the intensity of feeling among many segments of the population in a good part of the world against information dependency and cultural domination in general.

The consequences of computer communications and transborder data flows have just begun to be seen as salient issues to the leaders of, and policy makers in, the developing nations.* The situation is changing and the source of the change is practical necessity. Computer systems and processes are being installed in many countries and the economic and social problems attendant on their use, applicability, and impact are now beginning to be experienced.

We do know that the spread of computer communications is not haphazard. It occurs because transnational companies require these services for their international operations. Supporting and representing the objectives of the transnational order, United States' informatics and foreign policy press for early operationalism of communication technology in the poor world, claiming that the new instrumentation will overcome informational and economic dependency.

The argument undeniably is attractive. Communications facilities *are* inadequate in the poor nations. Informational needs *are* great. Assistance *seems* to be one way of overcoming material and nonmaterial deprivation. Under what circumstance then, if any, can the new information technology and processes serve the needs of people—not corporations—and assist in the strengthening of communal autonomy?

The answer will differ from place to place, but one common factor is present in making an assessment. The use to which the new technology is put, and therefore its ultimate social value, depends greatly on the internal balance of social forces in the community. The presence of strong, popular social movements and organizations can influence the initial design, the timing of the installation,

*A Cuban study, *Mass Media: Technology, dependency and use*, (Havana, 1978), touched on these matters. The Final Report of the International Commission for the Study of Communication Problems (the McBride Commission), *Many voices, one world*, (1980), took up some of these issues also but only marginally. See Herbert I. Schiller, "Electronic utopias and structural realities,"in Cees Hamelink, Ed., *Communication in the eighties: A reader on the McBride Report* Rome: IDOC, 1980.

and the utilization of the new technology for social ends. * Without such social inputs, it is almost certain that the new technology will strengthen the prevailing system of authority and privilege and serve the design of a new international division of labor, establishing communication links that integrate, more tightly than ever, the poor world and its governing elites with the transnational corporate order.

It is the poor world's ruling, propertied elites' identification of *their* interests and *their* survival with the transnational corporate order that largely accounts for that order's successful penetration and domination of much of Africa, Asia, and Latin America. It explains too, the often seemingly schizoid behavior of the elites on these continents, who rail against imperialism at the same time as they snuggle up more closely to the subjects of their verbal assaults. Anti-imperialism, in many parts of the Third World, is a useful mechanism employed to keep the desperate masses of impoverished people pacified, and diverted from the local sources of their misery.

Yet, rhetorical as anti-imperialism often is, and recognized as such by the more sophisticated transnational interests, it cannot be entirely disregarded. It perpetuates the deep and widespread anti-imperialism of the people themselves, *which is genuine*. It consequently poses long-term, as well as immediate, questions of the viability of the transnational order. It feeds the tension and increases the instability that are pervasive in the Third World. It makes 'doing business' a continuing problem for transnational 'guests'. In the latters' multiplying encounters with the local elites, they are confronted with incessant demands, sometimes to placate the distressed masses, often, to increase the holdings and influence of the local administrators and governors.

Brazil's considerable efforts to achieve some independence in the information sphere are nicely illustrative of a class endeavor presented as a national undertaking. In 1978, the executive secretary of CAPRE, the State Coordinating Committee on Electronic Data Processing Activities (now abolished and replaced by the Special Secretariat of Informatics), saw the informational issue this way:

---

*In Australia, the trade union movement has been active in attempting to participate in the decision making incidental to the introduction of new technology.

A new form of colonialism and dominance has replaced ·old-style physical occupation and nations are only able to exert their political and socio-cultural independence if they become *economically inter-dependent* with the others. Joining this exclusive club becomes, therefore,one of the major goals of any Third World Nation. Under-standing, transferring/adaption, and eventually even developing certain technologies is a sine qua non condition in the quest . . . . Brazil is trying hard to overcome its underdevelopment and join the interdependent club.[24]

But becoming "economically interdependent" in the trans-national corporate system is not the same thing as becoming inde-pendent and achieving national sovereignty. The introduction and use of computer communications to become part of the "exclusive club" may be given a nationalist complexion. [25] Yet the growth of a modern informational sector, undertaken with these objectives, can only strengthen the local entrepreneurial class, consolidate its position, extend its ties with external capital, widen its scope do-mestically, and promote its interests and values.

National informatics policy which accepts, or even insists, on in-terdependence, in practice, therefore, is entrepreneurial class pol-icy with a national flavor and language. A genuinely alternative course would look toward what Cees Hamelink terms "dissoci-ation"—a short to medium-term policy of disengagement, which would seek to afford a breathing space to national decision making, and allow indigenous needs to be formulated before embarking on developmental paths that carry unclear but powerful impera-tives.[26]

The strength of the popular sentiment against imperialism spills over into the international diplomatic sphere and creates additional problems for the transnational system. More than the active striv-ings of the transnational corporations, powerful as these are, is re-quired if international informational hegemony is to be obtained. In the face of deep and continent-wide anti-imperialism, an interna-tional legitimation of sorts is needed—much like the use that was made by the United States of the United Nations' Educational, Sci-entific, and Cultural Organization (UNESCO) in the early postwar period. UNESCO, it may be recalled, was one of the instruments chosen to propagate the "free flow of information" as a desirable universal, facilitating thereby the global expansion of American media conglomerates.

Now, unhappily for the transnational system, UNESCO, and
other international organizations that once effectively served
Western market system interests, have become 'politicized'. This
translates into refusing to follow automatically the policy positions
articulated by the few, core capitalist countries. Not too much
should be made of the reformist zeal of UNESCO, but even its mild
reluctance to accept unhesitatingly the dictates of its formerly unquestioned commanders is occasion for anger and outrage in Western centers. [27]

There is an urgent transnational corporate need, consequently,
for an international body in which anti-imperialism is muted and
where Western policy can be assured a respectful hearing, and,
more important, a fair prospect of implementation.

Morris H. Crawford, former executive director of the United
States Interagency Task Force as well as of the Advisory Group on
Transborder Data Flow, stated the case this way: There is "a
worldwide trend towards controlling information technology in
general and transborder data flows in particular. The US has enormous stakes in both." Where then should these matters be considered, and, if possible, their impact blunted? In the International
Telecommunications Union (ITU), for instance?

> ITU's charter does not extend, however, to computers. Enlarge-
> ment of its responsibilities is questioned by both the Secretariat as
> well as American corporations. The strong voice of the European
> PTTs [Postal and Telegraph Services] in ITU makes Americans
> think twice before giving ITU greater authority.

What about UNESCO? Again, Crawford's assessment is unenthu-
siastic.

> UNESCO, however, is not known to Americans for its cool and tem-
> pered debating. It is hardly a favored place for the complexities of in-
> formation technology and transborder data flows . . . . More and
> more Americans are worried by the restrictive policies that could
> hamper all information flows and cut them out of lucrative markets.
> They want to find out what is bothering other nations and do some-
> thing about it before it is too late. The Americans went to Rome [in
> June, 1980] for a look at IBI [Intergovernmental Bureau of In-
> formatics].[28]

The Intergovernmental Bureau of Informatics (IBI) began its
existence in 1951. Only in 1978 did it shed its low profile and begin

to become active in championing the worldwide expansion of telematics—the utilization and analysis of computer communications. Hosting two conferences, one in Torremolinos, Spain in 1978, and a second in Rome in 1980, the IBI has offered a meeting place and a forum for information industry contingents to address 62 national delegations, in Rome, about their plans to computerize the world. The delegates, in turn, have been able to express their hopes and apprehensions about these rapidly developing designs.

IBI sees itself as an organization defending the cultural and economic autonomy of Third World nations as they purchase and introduce advanced informational systems. It sees no contradiction between this objective and its own underlying assumption, one which emphasizes the necessity and desirabiliity of extending computer communications as rapidly as possible around the world, *regardless of the internal or external balance of social forces.*

It remains to be seen if the IBI can be used to facilitate the transnational corporate design for a new international division of labor. In any case, the American delegation to its 1980 Rome meeting apparently came away quite satisfied:

> In these circumstances, the Americans came away from Rome impressed, ready to take active roles in the working parties. They credit the meeting for an atmosphere of reason and open-minded receptivity. The Americans liked what they saw and heard in Rome.[29]

Yet the employment of *any* international organization for the task of imposing unequal relationships may already be beyond accomplishment.

The matters considered at the first IBI meeting in Torremolinos, in 1978, indicate why this may be so. The provisional agenda, reflecting the priorities of IBI's policymaking directorate, took for granted the proposition of moving ahead speedily with computer communications. However, it also was compelled to consider other issues, which could interfere with its number one objective. Some of these were:

> How to elaborate a list of national priorities in the application of informatics; how to assess and forecast the implications of introduction of newly emerging applications which require information networks and information utilities; which are the necessary measures to regulate those applications which might involve data flows through space or across national borders; which are the appropriate meas-

ures both in developing and developed countries to increase the confidence of the public and to benefit users of informatics, and to guard against the misuses of informatics technology.

How to determine the appropriateness of the informatics technology, software and hardware offered by the national and foreign manufacturers;how too formulate policy to develop an appropriate industrial infrastructure for informatics to ensure a partial or total technological independence in the key sectors of the national economy.[30]

This bundle of issues reveals the ambiguities and contradictions that permeate the IBI, and are just as likely to accompany any efforts, in any international forum, to establish a program completely acceptable to the transnational corporate system.

At Torremolinos, the overall goal of the transnational system, to get on quickly with the development and operation of global computer communications, was fused with the rest of the world's desire for protection *against* the unchecked power of that system. This combination of incompatibilities remains unresolved. It is likely to continue in this state of tension for some time to come because there is not adequate strength on either side—transnational or anti-imperialist–to decide the issue permanently.

If the Third World and other dependent states accept the new communication technology, they are clamped into an unequal relationship *at the outset*, vis à vis the transnational system. Yet the latter, though getting its way insofar as finding markets quickly for its products and processes, seems likely to be faced, also, with a multiplicity of new restrictions that limit its objective of uninhibited exploitation and profit making.

Some of the resolutions and recommendations adopted at the Torremolinos Conference give a sense of what these restrictions entail. For example, national plans for informatics were advanced which decried the United States' monopoly of data banks; the establishment of a world software bank was proposed; the creation of national centers for information hardware and software maintenance were recommended; international standards for computer communication technology systems were demanded; the scrutiny and regulation of transborder data flows were acknowledged to be necessary; and, overall, it was concluded that technology transfer, in general, should be subject to review and safeguards.

In practically all of the 43 resolutions adopted at the conference, recognition of, and concern with, existing power disparities were evident. Representative of this outlook was recommendation 41, which read in part:

> The SPIN conference [was]:
>
> Convinced that any dependence in the realm of informatics could give rise to a host of servitudes which should place the attributes of national sovereignty in jeopardy. . . .
>
> Aware of the commercial practices of certain transnational corporations which operate to the disadvantage of developing countries. . . .
>
> Recommends that UNESCO, in close collaboration with the Commission on Transnational Corporations and the United Nations Centre on Transnational Corporations, introduce a programme to strengthen the negotiating position of all countries, and particularly of developing countries, with regard to transnational corporations.[31]

Two years later, in Rome in 1980, the same mix of assertiveness on behalf of national sovereignty and acquiescence in arrangements that could undercut the possibilities for achieving informational equality and autonomy was present.

What can be concluded from this admittedly contradictory evidence of Third World acceptance and resistance to the transnational system's program for a new international division of labor? The balance sheet shows this relationship of forces: the weakness of most of the poor countries in the world; the strength of the transnational corporate system; and the opportunity of this system to further divide and weaken the majority of poor countries by fostering local entrepreneurial classes.

Taken by itself, this accounting would seem to indicate the near certain attainment, relatively soon, of the transnational corporate design for an new international division of labor—one in which the poor nations remain indefinitely in unfavorable positions. Even the increasing competition between the North American center and the Western European and Japanese enclaves of advanced industrialization, though possibly conferring some options and bargaining opportunities on the rest of the world, is ultimately a struggle at the top of the world power pyramid. The informatics networks now being established may strengthen United States, or German, or

Japanese, or possibly French controllers. But what happens in the remaining four-fifths of the world?

Still, the balance sheet may not be as one-sided as the *visible* forces now indicate it is. What cannot be left out of the calculation, but which also cannot be easily estimated or predicted, is *the resistance of people* to the massive dislocations and upheavals and the threats to human solidarity that already are being experienced in the course of creating a new international division of labor, fashioned by the transnational corporate system.

In the Third World, the existence of longstanding, and still strong, anti-imperialist feeling throughout the population is a force of enormous potential in the oncoming confrontations. It is the basis, it would seem, for the remarks of Dr. Rein Turn, chairman of the American Federation of Information Processing Societies' (Afips) panel on transborder data flow:

> The U.S. is likely to be faced with an altered economic reality. With controls on international information flows increasing, no longer will U.S. international enterprises (both information processing industries and other industries or enterprises) be able to continue the growth of their international operations and expansion in the same way they have to date. . . .
>
> These issues and the changes that will stem from them do not represent a temporary aberration in international relations; rather, they represent the beginning of a significant alteration in the present international economic order for informatics now dominated by First World Countries, the U.S. in particular.[32]

In the next section the center of the transnational system itself comes under scrutiny. In the United States, too, the people's resistance is a determining element in affecting the kind of new international division of labor that may be expected in the time ahead.

DEVELOPMENTS IN THE CORE AREA: TRANSFORMATIONAL PROSPECTS IN THE UNITED STATES

The challenges and demands that have just been examined, and that confront the United States in its efforts to use information technology (and information) as the levers to manage a new international divison of labor, are all externally based. That is, they are pressures originating *outside* of the United States. Now the heartland itself must be evaluated for its ability to introduce and administer the changes that are creating a new, hierarchical, global order of domination—one based on information technology and its products.

What are and what will be the reactions inside the United States to the massive changes that are looming—some already underway? Put differently, how secure is the base on which a global structure of computer communications is being constructed? For a full estimate, economic, technological, social, and psychological elements in the domestic economy would have to be considered and measured. In this section, only employment, work relations, and personal security will be reviewed, and these only briefly. Still, these may be sufficient to indicate the fragility and instability which now are the main characteristics of the center of the world market system.

In the fall of 1980, the editors of *Computerworld*, the weekly newspaper which reports computer developments in the United States, spoke at length with James Martin, "the foremost authority on the social and commercial impact of computers." Martin states at the very beginning of the interview that in the 1980s, "we're going to change almost everybody's job." This will mean "mass deplacement," not mass unemployment, Martin hastens to add, because people will have the opportunity to move up to "jobs which are more demanding."

Not everybody sees these developments this way, Martin admits. The public persists in having a "dim perception of these changes." The mass media must be employed to change this outlook, with a message, Martin believes, that should run something like this:

> One of the things we've got to say to them (the public) is, in the long run everything is *probably going to turn out OK; with good things as well as* bad things, and the good things will predominate. But on the way we're going to have to make a lot of changes which will be *temporarily* uncomfortable, like running out of petroleum.[33]

The seismic changes in the economy that Martin and others predict will occur in the next two decades, are—it is our contention, repeated throughout this work—almost completely the consequences of decisions and nondecisions of the *Fortune 500*. This makes it al-

most inevitable, that, similar to the experiences of the first industrializing process more than a century and a half ago in England
(and then in the United States), those in command of this new phase
of development will attempt to push most, if not the entire burden
of the enormous costs, onto the working population. The important
difference is that times are not the same, in the United States and
in the rest of the world.

In *Computerworld's* dialogue with James Martin, this question is
asked:

> By some overly pessimistic estimates, from 50% to 75% of all
> U.S.factory workers could be replaced by smart robots by the end of
> the century. Office workers, too, wonder if word processors and au-
> tomation will replace them even sooner. Is a confrontation between
> labor and management over automation inevitable at the bargaining
> table? What is the possible outcome of such a confrontation?

Once again, the matter comes down to the reactions of people to the
developments taking place. Martin gives this reply: "We're certainly going to have a confrontation at the bargaining table. The
question is, how bad does it become?"[34]

Martin is reasonably confident that it will be manageable because
trade unionists will see that among other benefits, there is a long
run value in eliminating disagreeable work. However forward-
looking in engineering affairs, when faced with social questions
Martin accepts and works within a limited traditional framework.

If, in fact, enormous changes and losses in the jobs available in
the next 20 years do occur, what reason is there to believe and trust
in negotiations at the bargaining table with the sort of labor leaders
that have occupied the scene over the last 30 years?

Developments such as these may not be a matter for quiet, or
even argumentative discussion. The issues may be contested at the
plantsites and in the street, by social movements that today are nowhere visible, in popular coalitions that will bring together 'displaced' workers, students never employed, women and minorities
laid off at the outset of 'productivity-increasing' programs, and
other groupings that find the corporate-directed technological
order distressing, physically intolerable, and socially repressive. If
the beginning of the industrial revolution had its opposition, and it
did, the new electronics transformations may introduce a totally
new dimension of resistance.

The worksite itself may become one locus of opposition. Consider the future work scene in an extensively computerized society outlined by Dr. Carl Hammer, director of computer sciences for Sperry UNIVAC. As the number of computers and people employed in computer jobs increase, Hammer foresees an overriding concern with the security of data. He predicts that it will become a "privilege" to work in a data processing environment. Accordingly, "if you want to work there you will have to agree to work under surveillance."

People will have to become accustomed to working under an "assumption of guilt." Outside the clean, information worksites, growing numbers of "displaced" workers will congregate. Inside, another unreliable element—the disgruntled employee. And, Hammer notes, "Everybody is a disgruntled employee more or less." So, "in Hammer's words—'a Nazi-like system may be a prerequisite for this type of employment'.[35] Outside the workplace, in the community at large, apprehension about the range of control of personal lives the computer enables supervisory ranks to exercise already is pervasive. Public uneasiness and suspicion about the new electronic technology is a continuing source of worry to information industry leaders. An IBM executive voices a frequently expressed view: "We're going to have to work very hard to overcome the public's distrust of the computer, distrust of technology."[36]

A survey of public attitudes to computers, undertaken by Louis Harris & Associates in 1978 and reported in *Datamation*, revealed a great and growing popular doubt and worry about computers' impact on personal privacy. Two-thirds of the public polled, believed the computer should be restricted for privacy, while only 8 percent of computer executives thought this was necessary. *Datamation's* writer's conclusion is:

> The survey offers a warning to the computer industry, computer users, and public policy makers. The privacy issue is not solved and fading away. It is going to become more intense in the next decade as "privacy" serves as the handle with which a still considerably alienated public seeks to define and install greater measures of individual or social control over an organizational system whose powers have been vastly increased by computer uses in the last 20 years.[37]

Here is another indication that the popular will is still to be heard from and *will be expressed in the future*. These still-limited oppositional sentiments, in time, may be joined with the demands of those caught in the 'displacement' crunch. Also, still to be taken into account are the reactions of those working within the tightening security nets cast over the informational enterprise.

Left entirely out of this discussion, but of unmistakable relevance, are other, very powerful, sources of potential breakdown in the overall economy. A few of the more visible ones can be specified: the continuing, astronomical deficits in the United States' foreign trade; the unchecked price inflation; the unyielding, high unemployment; the incredibly overextended debt of the consumer and private sector alike; and the chemical despoliation and ecological disrepair of the national living space. Accompanying, or perhaps issuing from, these sectors of economic malfunctioning, is the malaise in the social sphere, which is a matter of daily reportage and personal encounter.

Despite the non-stop operation of the powerful, social conditioning machinery—the outpourings of the 'leisure-entertainment' conglomerates and the 24-hour 'news' services— a revival of political action directed toward radical, systemic change seems a strong prospect. Social conflict in the core of the transnational corporate system is the forecast for tomorrow. This being so, the new international division of labor may find its strongest opposition, paradoxically enough, in its privileged center.

Notes to Chapter Eight

1.   John Eger, "Information, informatics, and international information flows: Predicates for new world law and policy," paper given at the symposium *World Communications: Decision for the Eighties*, Annenberg School of Communication, University of Pennsylvania, Philadelphia, May 12–14, 1980

2.   Bertram Gross, *Friendly fascism*. New York: Evans, 1980

3.   "European society; faced with the challenge of new information technologies: A community response," Commission of the European Communities, COM (79) 650 final Brussels, November 26, 1979, pp. 10–12, emphasis added.

4.   Sachio Senmoto, "Transnational communication enterprises and national communication policies based on new technologies," paper presented at the Communication Institute, East-West Center, Honolulu, August 6–19, 1978.

5.   *Computerworld*, May 5, 1980, p. 66.

6.   Bohdan O. Szuprowicz, "France leading services supplier in Europe," *Computerworld*, September 8, 1980, p. 81.

7.   S. Nora & A. Minc, *L'Informatisation de la societe (The informatisation of society)*, Documentation Francaise, Paris, 1978.

8.   Christian D'Aumale, French Ambassador to the OECD, address to the Intergovernmental Bureau of Informatics, Data Flow Conference, Rome, 1980. Reprinted in *Transnational Data Report*, July/August 1980, *3* (3/4). pp. 29-31.

9.   Marcia Blumenthal, "French flag waves behind DP industry," *Computerworld*, October 15, 1979, Also, "French technology plans," *The New York Times*, October 3, 1980, p. 87.

10. *Nora & Minc, op. cit.*

11. DIANE News, March 1980, (18).

12. *Ibid.*

13. Arthur L. Robinson, "Perilous times for U.S. microcircuit makers," *Science*, May 9, 1980, *208*, pp. 582–586

14. Charles P. Llecht, "Tsunami," *Computerworld*, June 5, 1978, p. 89.

15. John Tagliabue, "Bonn said to press German city not to buy computer from U.S.," *The New York Times*, October 4, 1980, p. 31.

16. Rossiter W. Langhorne, "Transborder data flow: Should it be regulated?", *Computerworld*, October 30, 1978, pp. 70–71.

17. Geza Feketskuty, before the U.S. House of Representatives' Subcommittee on Government Information and Individual Rights, April 21, 1980. Reprinted in *Transnational Data Report*, September 1980, *3 (5) p. 7.*

18. Jan Freese, Symposium on Transborder Data Flows and Protection of Privacy: Impacts and Trends. Vienna, September 20–23, 1977. Organization of Economic Co-Operation and Development (OECD), Summary Report, DSTI/ICCP/77.47, December 12, 1977, Paris, p. 39.

19. J. M. Treille, *Ibid.*, p. 24.

20. Morris Crawford, "The Vienna Symposium," United States State Department Washington, D.C., 1977, mimeo.

21. Kathleen Casey, "Transborder data flows," background paper for consideration by members of the Subcommittee on Communications, Committee on Interstate and Foreign Commerce, U.S. House of Representatives, Washington, D.C., October 3, 1977, pp. 21–22.

22. "The debate on transborder data flows," *EDP Analyzer*, April 1978, *16* (4), p. 10. And advertising, the vital force of advanced capitalism, is dependent totally on access to audience information (de-

mographics), for the pinpointed transmission of its mostly transnational marketing messages.

23.   G. Russell Pipe, "International treaty on data protection, privacy, in limbo," *Computerworld*, January 28, 1980, p.20.

24.   Ricardo A. C. Saur, "Informatics, new technologies and data regulation: A view from the Third World," in *Data regulation: European and Third World realities*. Uxbridge, England: 1978 Online, pp. 223–233, emphasis added.

25.   Ney Seara Kruel, "Brazil's DPers solidify national policy stance," *Computerworld*, November 20, 1978, p. 10. Also, Joubert De Oliveira, Executive Secretary of the Special Secretariat of Informatics, Address before the IBI Meeting in Rome, 1980, *Transnational Data Report, July/August 3* (3/4) pp.32-34.

26.   Cees Hamelink, *Third World and cultural emancipation*. Forthcoming.

27.   Gerald Long, the managing director of Reuters Ltd. news agency, for example, speaks of UNESCO's "michievous and dangerous activities in the news area." Alan Otten, "Fight over proper role of mass media could flare anew at UNESCO meeting," *The Wall Street Journal*, September 19, 1980.

28.   Morris H. Crawford, "The IBI transborder data flow conference: An American view," *Transnational Data Report*, July/August 1980, *3* (3/4), p. 38.

29.   *Ibid.*

30.   Annotated Provisional Agenda, SPIN Conference, 1978, Inter-Governmental Conference on Strategies and Policies of Informatics, Torremolinos (Spain), August 23–September 6, 1978, UNESCO/SC-78 SPIN/1/Add. IBI/SPIN/GR/151/Add., Paris, May 31, 1978, pp. 2–3.

31.   Recommendations Approved by the Spin Conference. News letter No. 27, 1978, 4th Quarter, Intergovernmental Bureau for Informatics, Rome, Italy.

32.   Rein Turn, "Transborder data flow,"*Computerworld*, March 3, 1980, "In Depth" Section.

33.   "At home with James Martin," *Dawn of the Software Decade*, *Computerworld*, September 17, 1980, *14* (38), p. 17, emphasis added.

34.   *Ibid.*,p. 29.

35.   Jake Kirchner, "'Nazi techniques' envisioned for DP security," *Computerworld*, April 14, 1980, p. 14.

36.   Jake Kirchner, "Design systems for amateurs, IBMer suggest," *Computerworld*, September 22, 1980, p. 25.

37.   Alan F. Westin, "The impact of computers on privacy," *Datamation*, December 1979, pp. 190–194.

Author Index

Subject Index